Wence Horak

DEEPER GREEN

CRUX EDITION

OTHER BOOKS BY THE AUTHOR:

ANCIENT ECOLOGISTS   (an e-book and paperback)
SKY GODS AND ANGELS   (an e-book and paperback)
/OR OUR ANCESTORS RETURN FROM SPACE TO EARTH/
NOSTRADAMUS DECODED   (an e-book and paperback)

Published by
Earth Way
P.O. Box 24033
Kelowna, B.C. V1Y 9H2
Canada

ISBN 978-1-989068-01-4 e-book
ISBN 978-1-989068-00-7 paperback

TABLE OF CONTENTS

INTRODUCTION

Science, in order to be 'real science', requires the element of predictability. Since climatology lacked this feature, it embraced the idea of the Serbian mathematician Milutin Milankovitch, he came up with almost 100 years ago. It asserts, based on the geometrical dance of Earth around the Sun, the periodic alterations of 10,000 years long interglacials and 90,000 years long glacial periods, with Darwinistically gradual transitions from one to the other.

And, of course, since it was officially acknowledged the planet is warming up, during the first 20 years the temperature increases were barely noticeable, as if in compliance with the theory. This encouraged the climatologists in believing it will continue in this trend, in spite the known records pointing to the opposite, and they, along with the politicians, kept repeatedly assuring the public, saying: "We have time to fix this," and "Somehow, we shall pull through, as we always do."

But when the climate induced weather started to hit some extreme notes, and when even the IMF chairwoman Christine Lagarde commented, "We are going to be toasted, roasted and grilled," they went into panic mode. The result of that was the Paris Agreement, signed in December 2015 by politicians from 195 countries, that pledges to prevent the global temperature from rising by no more than 2°C, preferably by no more than 1.5°C. And towards this end the developing countries were promised $100 million a year in aid. At this stage, there is very little evidence this promise is actually being fulfilled.

But even if it were, the goal set up by this Agreement simply was not achievable, as was pointed out by people with relevant qualifications, like James Hansen, contributors to the journal Nature, etc. They concluded that even when spending that kind of money, the global temperature would still rise by 3°C, and thus deliver a runaway global warming. To prevent that would require massive carbon dioxide extraction from the atmosphere, using unproven or non-existent technologies, at an annual cost of $12 to $60 trillion. Yet, the global revenues are just around $20trillion, with a lot of deficits.

But if that was the case, why did I bother to write this book, you might ask, since our goose is roasted anyhow. And my answer is the book itself. It will reveal that 'things' are not as they seem, or as the Neo-Darwinists think they are.

As you will find out, the main focus of this book is to rectify, where needed, the current concepts of reality, while explaining as much as possible, that our evolution, which is much, much longer than we are led to believe, was always about ecology, about the importance of living on a forested planet, under ice age conditions, and about the size of the human population inhabiting it. And while some of the prehistoric people were aware of this, and tried to protect the planet as long as they were able to, they ultimately failed, because it was our fate to experience what we are about to, in order to complete our evolution.

While such a claim will sound dubious to people imbedded in the currently prevailing dogma of accidental universe, and of evolution based on the competitive "survival of the fittest," other, equally scientific concepts, but a lot more open-minded, vehemently disagree with it, for which they are accorded either silence or disrespect, by the reigning and financially supported body of the Neo-Darwinists.

To be as brief as possible here, I will only mention David Bohm, the quantum physicist who, decades ago, observed that "the universe is evolving with a purpose, towards a goal." It was also he who named universe the Cosmic Being. A few years back, another physicist, Paul Davies, published an article in which he explained the universe had to know the entire future, even before it emerged, and that it had enough calculating capacity to carry out the required steps. And as the mathematical models demonstrate, the processes involved in the formation of the 'material' universe, and of the life within it, indeed defy mathematical odds, making it obvious neither could be here by accident.

When it comes to life, or the 'stuff' it is made of, it is equally plain this cannot be the result of competition, but only of co-operation, as first suggested by biologist Lynn Margulis. This is evident in the structure of atoms, of living cells, of body organs, of entire ecosytems, and of the living organisms that compromise it, forming the complex body of life on Earth.

However, every form of life is vulnerable, and needs protection in form of an immune system. Every living cell has one, every living body – except the body of Earth. And surprise, surprise, mankind is supposed to become "it," the immune system of their native planet.

Of course, questions would arise, how could a species, now demonstrably destroying the planet, become its protector. And the answer to that is over one million years long, which is how long our real evolution took, as can be fairly accurately gleaned from myths that speak of five preceding cycles of civilizations, most in general terms, some in surprising details. Yet, what should not be a surprise is they all self-destructed by devastating the planet. Also, it would seem the first two cycles, in existence sometimes between 1.2 million and 800,000 years ago, ruined it more than the following two, implying a learning process. We can even say that the species who destroyed it the most, just over 25,000 years ago, was not even our species, but a more ancient race of giants, whose existence was long denied by anthropologists, until the recent discoveries in Australia.

This also suggests that it is always a minority of the Earth's population that is aware of the climate conditions required for our existence on the planet, and the fairly narrow limits for it. And this likely led to the conditions under which our cycle of civilizations evolved.

The Ice Age ended suddenly and cataclysmically, some 15,500 years ago, devastating the planet so completely, it had to be terraformed by generations of descendants of the survivors. They had spent 3,600 years at this task when, around 11,700 years ago, all the carbon dioxide and methane, accumulated in the atmosphere, triggered a hellish heat spike, that drove the global temperature past 24°C, for about 1,500 years.

It was during this period our Cro-Magnon craniums, containing, on average, some 1,650 cc of brain, got reduced by circa 20 percent. This, the 'experts' started to realize only recently, but are unable to guess when or why, in spite multiple evidence, found in ancient sources, relevant to the time.

The next surprise is the claim, made by the same sources, that until about 12,000 years ago, people were able to receive communications from the Cosmic Being, likely via the quantum computers in our (brain) cells, known as microtubules. The information they received concerned mankind's fate over the next 12,000 difficult years, and it was dutifully maintained by a number of organizations dedicated to such a purpose, until the Roman times, but parts of it survived till the present.

These records tell us that mankind will, again, ravage the planet, but this time we will be saved, in "the nick of time," by a circa 1.5 kilometer asteroid, impacting in the Artic. This, and its consequences, will then trigger a new ice age, as such always deliver the optimum conditions for all life. A proof of that will be the transformation of our craniums back to the Cro-Magnon size, or 25 percent increase over the current norm, starting with the generation that will be born 40 years after the impact.

However, this act will not be saving the entire extant mankind, but mostly just the current minority that is, in most ways, living their lives the way people were always meant to, whether they know it or not. As for the rest, there is the sentence in the Bible, repeated there several times, in which God says, "I will destroy those who destroy Earth." Perhaps even more surprisingly, this God also sees deserts turned into forests, once His Kingdom is established on Earth.

Since the asteroid is expected during a lunar occlusion in December, I would hazard a guess it will be in 2020 or 2021. Any later dates would likely be too late for most of the large animals, as 2/3 of them could be extinct by around 2020, in the wild. Most of the others would follow quickly, all due to the ever growing human population, that craves the land where they live, their meat, or other body parts, like ivory.

But the Earth cannot support, endlessly, anyhow, the projected human population of 9 or 10 billion, or even the current population of circa 7.5 billion. Certainly not at the Western living standards, as these countries use up several times the resources that each of them has. And, as the Club of Rome people projected quite correctly, way back in 1973, that the atmospheric carbon dioxide will rise to 370 PPM, by the year 2000, they also projected, in their standard model, that the availability of food, per capita, and of the non-renewable resources, would steeply decline, by around 2025. And, as far as the human population the planet is able to support indefinitely, the estimates talk of around one billion, or less.

In the closing note I need to express my suspicion that even most of those who consider themselves Green do not know there were people a lot more dedicated than they are to preserving not just what we call "environment," but the very viability of our planet, to the point of sacrificing their lives for it, long millennia ago, and ages before that, and that they all need to know more about the past and about the future. For this reason the book is titled Deeper Green, and in this sense it is dedicated to those willing to be Deeper Greens, and to their future. A future they must individually earn by co-operating with other like-minded people, or lose it.

ANCIENT ROOTS

Most people, including the Green Party members and ecologists, think that concern for ecology and taking care of the Earth are very modern ideas. In fact, these are very ancient ideas and we would not be here without the people who practiced both, as the myths tell us.

Our historical period starts with the termination of the last Ice Age, some 15,500 years ago. As to how fast it took place, modern estimates range from years to mere weeks, within which the bulk of the ice cover collapsed. During this apocalypse of mega-storms, monster tidal waves overtopped Mount Orohena, according to a Tahitian myth, which is 2,241 m high. When the elements were done with the planet, all the forests were destroyed, huge marshes and bogs formed inland, as all the rivers got clogged up, and only 29,000 people had survived, according to ancient 'myths'.

In the meantime, the huge volumes of ice super-cooled the oceans, and these, in turn, cooled down the atmosphere, which led to a partial but substantial reglaciation.

Yet, the bulk of climatologists, under the influence of the Darwinian dogma of extremely slow changes, reinforced by the equally dubious Milenkovitch theory, see this zig zag process as gradual melting. The funny thing is, the myths, whose authors were there, contradict the climatologists.

The two most obvious examples are found among the Tamil myths, of India, and among the Sumerian myths. One Tamil 'myth' tells us a university was founded, shortly after the flood, then terminated three times by subsequent heat waves and floods. These we will date later. The Sumerian 'myth' of Atrahasis tells us our ancestors had been working on saving the planet by digging out new river channels, to drain the inland bogs and marshes, and by planting continents with forests, for 3,600 years, before they were forced to abandon their labors. To survive, people had to quickly migrate to the northern polar region, as is also vaguely alluded to in an ancient Egyptian text, as well as in the presence of Dravidian and Czech words and grammar in Siberian languages. The "forcing agent" was the tremendous heat wave that gripped the Earth, starting some 11,700 years ago, during which, the climatologist claim, the global temperature soared by 7°C. This is clearly contradicted by a Hittite myth of the Vanished God (of Rain), that plainly tells us it was so hot, no mammals, including people, were able to procreate. This, as is fairly well-known, can happen only when the global temperature exceeds 24°C, or 11°C warmer than is the 'norm'. This, nowadays, is given as 13°C.

This heat spike was terminated, circa 10,200 years ago, by an impact of a large, fragmented asteroid, which some say was originally 10 km in size, that impacted along the Carolinas' shores.

However, to the shock of the people, expressed in numerous myths and ancient texts, during this heat spike human cranium got reduced by 20 percent, which resulted in the loss of circa 50 percent of our neural connections. Yet, there are also indications this process took place in three stages, including the two subsequent warm-ups, circa 7,200 and 4,350 years ago. Both were accompanied by global floods, and both were terminated by asteroid impacts. One circa 5,200 years ago in the Antarctic and the last one, some 4,000 years ago, in the Sahara.

In either case, the cranial reduction afflicted the males a lot more critically, which ushered in the Age of Matriarchy, still clearly evident in the Indian epics and, what we deem to be, Celtic myths. These societies, ruled by Amazon queens, all operated under the umbrella of the (so called) Bear Cult philosophy.

Its main goal, again, was to maintain the viability of the planet, by planting a lot of forests, most of which were destroyed during the heat spike. This activity is confirmed in Celtic and Seneca Indian myths, that clearly talk about forests where trees grow in straight lines. Hardly a natures' way of propagating these.

The Bear Cult's main goddess was Artemis, whom the Romans had reduced to a quaint goddess of hunt, while the original one was mainly the goddess of the forest, and all those who lived there, even in China, under the name of Quan Yin, or Grandmother Forest. But if she was known as huntress, it is because she, or rather the Bear Cult members, 'hunted' the people. Not to eat them, but to drive them out of their forests, which they started to destroy, by slash and burn technique, to create pastures and fields, or just to live off the Bear Cult labours. This too is described in the Celtic myths and Indian epics.

In fact, we can thank only the Amazon queens and their Bear Cult, which armed their men exclusively for the military actions, for preserving the life on this planet, at the cost of eradicating entire kingdoms of invaders, who were breeding like rabbits, and kept devouring ever more forested land.

The speed of procreation is illustrated in the Irish legend about the first people to settle there. When they arrived, they numbered only 49 people, yet, 300 years later, they numbered 50,000. At that stage a new wave of migrants arrived, carrying with them a virus that killed all the natives. Had they lived, in another 300 years there would have been, theoretically, 500,000 of them, give or take.

This, however, also invalidates the anthropologists' claims of perennially low human population. If anything, it seems to suggest the population of the planet, even in the remote past, was going up and down like the proverbial yo-yo, regulated not just by the Bear Cult, but by the very climatic changes the surges in population had triggered.

We know it started to warm up, rather dramatically, again about 7,200 years ago, with the global temperature shooting up by at least 3°C, and the sea level surged by circa 40 metres. While we see no evidence of any major population fluctuations in Europe, North America was devastated. As the archeologists tell us, the southern part of the U.S. was so desiccated, only a few small bands of natives survived there, wandering from one drinking hole to another. In Manitoba, it was likely the dust storms, and the absence of wild animals, that drove the natives beyond the Polar Circle.

However, when the asteroid impacted in the Antarctic, some 5,200 years ago, it got so cold in Europe the locals, in order to keep warm, chopped down all the trees in the inhabited elevated locations of Central Europe, which led to massive soil erosion and to the silting up of rivers there. As a result they had to shift south-east to southern Ukraine. Yet, only a few centuries later it got rather warm again, and the proto-Europeans were back on their old home ground, to the surprise of the local archaeologist, as they realized the entire region must have been miraculously reforested, and the clogged-up rivers cleared out, but they did not know how.

The same scenario got repeated after the asteroid impact, some 4,000 years ago, in the Sahara. This time though, being a lot more numerous, some of the proto-Europeans settled in Greece, some in today's Turkey, where they became known as the Hittites, some marched on to become Persians, some parked it in Afghanistan, others, the so called Aryans, went to India, while still others, who eventually became the Germanic people, ended up wandering the southern belt of Siberia, for about 1,500 years.

But while the majority of the proto-Europeans remained on the north shore of the Black Sea, a permanent low pressure settled between Hungary and Sicily, over which area it rained and rained between 1,200 to 1,100 BCE, while the rest of Europe and the Near East were bone dry. This dislodged them from their temporary habitats, and sent them, under the name of the Sea Peoples, to attack Troy and the Hittite Empire, and by marching through and sailing by the Middle East, to invade Egypt. Twice defeated, most of them made a U-turn and headed back for Central Europe. There the forests stood again, in their mature majesty, and clean streams and rivers were flowing between secure banks – thanks to the Bear Cult.

The Cult likely had remained a viable social force there until the Germanic tribes, who snuck back in, from their 1,500 year long sojourn, around 500 BCE, were dislodged from their new homes in Denmark, by a measly sea level rise of about 1.5 meter, and started pouring onto the continent around 150 BCE. And peculiarly enough, it was only the British archeologist, excavating Carthage, who found that out, which also forced them to realize that was the reason why Romans were able to take the city. The water was simply high enough for their ships to sail over the heavy chain, barring the entrance into the harbour.

So, this minimal sea level rise, while unknown to the climatologist, had helped to doubly reaffirm the future history of Europe. It removed the Carthagians from the picture and put the Germanic people there. But the reason the climatologists did not see this blimp in their ice cores is simple: it was not there, having melted away. This had set off an alarm in my mind long time ago, but only recently I realized how sensitive the global climate must be, because during the second century BCE it gradually warmed up by only 1°C to 1.5°C, as supported by reports of numerous sunken ships from that period in the Mediterranean, and of vicious storms that occurred there for centuries.

The topic of one missing ice core layer though brings us to the reliability of the ice cores as indicators of the past climatic periods, since these represent the major tool for their dating.

As we have duly noted here, the extremely hot spell lasted some 1,500 years, the second, and still very warm spell, lasted about 2,000 years, while the last one was perhaps 400 years long, with the global temperature always substantially higher then today. But even with the temperature comparable to today, the glaciers melted enough to raise the sea level by up to 1.5 m. In other words, the ice cores, especially those from Greenland, must be missing about 4,000 years worth of data.

Yes, the climatologists, if only in a certain sense though, started to catch on, but for now, in order to maintain their faith, they are talking about incursion of older carbon dioxide into the younger layers, which would be hard to do, impossible in fact, by any natural means.

What this all boils down to is not only the reliability of climatic and other scientific data in general, but reliability of all scientific predictions and theories, such as the evolution of life, based on the Darwinian dogma of slow, gradual changes, backed up by the ongoing attempts, especially by American scientist, to make the facts fit the theory.

Part of the problem is, all branches of science, including climatology, got infected by the predictability bug, as they feel that without this feature they would not be deemed real sciences, and thanks to this thinking, climate is now deemed an incremental system, when in fact it is a chaotic one, and thus, by its very nature, it's behaviour, when put under stress, is unpredictable. The system, of course, will attempt to maintain a status quo for a certain time, but when pushed too far for too long, it will flip suddenly, as we know it did already four times, over the last 15,000 plus years.

But the only place where you see this key issue discussed is on the web, where people are asking the same question and answering the same way I would: "It's the job, stupid." Yet, it has to be admitted that the 2014 report by the American Association for the Advancement of Science spelled out that fact as well, and it is also claimed that even the IPCC had admitted, years ago, the climate is a chaotic system and its long-term future cannot be predicted by any means. So much then for the long-term projections of climate change and global temperature rise. More details on that in subsequent chapters.

THE STATE OF OUR PLANET

The current political flavour of the climate change discussion is the Paris Agreement, which would like to keep the global temperature from rising by no more than 1.5°C to 2°C above the pre-industrial level, and they all assume the airs of seriousness talking about it, while, at the same time, the powers that be talk about expanding the economy and of increasing energy production by 150 percent by 2050. Well, good luck magicians.

In the meantime, the global temperature jumped by circa 0.3°C in 2016 alone, to 1.4°C, which is the beginning of the 21st-century, not its end. This also means the Amazon forest can start burning in 2020, instead of 2030, and with most of it gone, the atmospheric column above the Earth, already down by about 10 percent, will start diminishing ever faster. The problem is, that 'forest' alone absorbs about 20 percent of the CO2 and produces a lot of the planet's oxygen, according to estimates.

The rapidly rising temperature will also speed up melting of the permafrost and the release of methane, that is at least 20 odd times more potent as the greenhouse gas than carbon. And while these two factors alone would guarantee a runaway greenhouse effect, a third factor, hidden in the sky, would then totally ruin the civilization.

That factor is called global dimming which, in spite of the high level of greenhouse gases in the atmosphere, the ground level temperature stays about 1.5°C cooler, although some say up to 3°C cooler, thanks to the aerosol particles from jet engines, but also to the sulphate and soot in the atmosphere, put there by heavy industries. The problem with the dimming effect is that its details are too complex, like everything connected to ecology, for scientist to be sure about the facts, and in this case they admit it. Usually, this is one way of saying the dimming affect could be greater. Now, that we started to reduce or eradicate these factors, the global temperature started to rise more noticeably, and we also have to keep in mind that the Earth, all told, is about 3°C warmer by now, while we keep pumping out more greenhouse gases.

Furthermore, the geniuses who originated the Paris Agreement, and who signed up on it, either did not read the last article George Monbiot had ever written about the climate change for *The Guardian,* or they do not really care. In this article, for which his scientist colleagues at Oxford University provided the specific details, he demonstrated that even taking all possible measures to reduce the greenhouse gases in the UK, or anywhere else for that matter, would never be enough to prevent further warming. The key reason, he never mentioned, are people.

It is no secret that people exhale carbon dioxide, the main ingredient of global warming, so far, but out of social correctness this fact remains taboo, even if it is fairly easy to calculate. In my estimation, the 7.5 billion people currently alive produce about 4 billion tons of carbon dioxide a year, or roughly 10 percent of the circa 40 billion tons produced currently.

To this we have to add other carbon dioxide sources directly tied to human existence, such as the domestic animals, that produce about 18 percent, rice fields, about 15 percent, and deforestation, about 17 percent, for a total of 60 percent. This, then, is the main reason why the count of atmospheric carbon dioxide now stands at 410 ppm, and going higher.

But, of course, the bean counters do not look at this, because they lack imagination, and knowledge of anything else but their beans, which they call facts. Yes, they too could calculate that a person at rest exhales circa 2.3 pounds of carbon dioxide a day, or just over 1 kg, for a total of about 40 billion tons a year, after you multiply it by 7.5 billion people. Then they turn around though, claiming not only that such a calculation is misleading, because we are merely reprocessing the carbon dioxide the plants produced, as if we were all vegetarians, each with our own little garden. This also is the reason why neither humans, nor the domestic animals are included in such calculations.

Yes, such arguments do have some credit, but only with the human population of the planet at a stone age level, at less than one billion. After all, we are the top predators, and the basic rule of nature requires that predators have to be a tiny minority. Breaking that rule means starvation, and/or extinction.

The catch is, while the herbivores existence is carbon neutral, the same, obviously, cannot be said about the predators eating them. When it comes to humans, the picture gets more complicated. If we ate only vegetables and fruits, or things made out of flour, we could remain carbon neutral. Problem is, all the stuff has to be harvested, transported, cooked or baked, which takes energy and labor. Furthermore, much of it is also processed and packaged, which consumes more of the same. I am also quite certain the vegetables and cereals, consumed by one person, do not absorb, during their short growing season, even a fraction of the carbons this person exhales.

The fact is, we had to cut forests to create fields or pastures, yet these absorb but a tiny fraction of carbon dioxide, compared to forests in temperate zones, and produce equally small amounts of oxygen.

Also, finally, the same experts, who claim our existence is carbon neutral, in fact claim we represent a "carbon sink," since human bodies contain about 18 percent carbon, by weight. At the same time, they remain mum as to what happens to all that carbon after we die. Still, even that amount, or circa 170 kg of carbon dioxide per capita, is negligible in comparison to the volume of it we exhale annually during our life-time, as noted.

The fatally wrong assumption that 'simple' presence of billions of people on Earth has no bearing on the changing climate can readily be demonstrated on the available historical evidence. The closest example to us, in time, is World War I. We know that, when it ended, in 1918, there were 320 ppm of carbon dioxide in the atmosphere. We also know that during that war some 20 million people got killed. Then the Spanish flu hit, which killed up to 100 million more people. As usual though, estimates vary, ranging from 50 to 100 million, yet even the estimates for individual countries, such as the U.S., very by almost 50 percent and for most, like China or India, do not exist at all. I am opting for the higher figure mainly in view of its ecological impact, as in the world that had a population of almost 1.9 billion, at the end of the war, the death of at least 100 million people, if we count all the victims, led to the sudden reduction of atmospheric carbon dioxide from 320ppm to 290 ppm, by the 1922 to 1923 period, or the 1870 level. That is circa 10 percent carbon dioxide drop for perhaps 6 percent population reduction.

In other words, there is direct evidence here, that the more people there are, the more needs they have, the more carbon dioxide goes into the atmosphere, while the reverse is true as well, and while the technological impact remained unchanged.

More of the same evidence is available from the entire period of the Little Ice Age, which is synonymous with incessant wars, mainly in Europe and China, where two of them eliminated about 50 percent of the population each, and waves of plagues, all over the (known) world, which also periodically eliminated 30 percent to 50 percent of (global) population. It was in fact these massive population losses that maintained the cool climate, which sometimes led to crop failures and more death by starvation.

Yet, in spite of all this the global population slowly grew, and once it had reached 1 billion, around 1850, the planet started to warm up, which can hardly be blamed on the presence of a few steam engines and the use of coal in the British fireplaces. As noted, the almost doubling of global population, between 1870 and 1918, added over 10 percent of carbon dioxide to the atmosphere.

And while allowing for a certain time lag, especially considering the incredible current burgeoning of the global population, there seems to be a direct correlation between the growth of the human population by one billion and the rise of atmospheric carbon dioxide by circa 30 ppm. We just need to acknowledge that, without the Spanish flu and both World Wars, the atmospheric carbon dioxide count would now stand around 450 ppm, instead of the current 410 ppm. Sadly, and perhaps counterintuitively, the industrial output plays but a lesser role.

It should not be all that surprising then to see similar surges took place a lot further back in time, as was also noted by Professor Ruddiman. This concerns the two periods of sudden warming and global floods, circa 7,200 and 4,350 years ago.

Since that again has a direct bearing on the global population level, we first have to address this concern. Regarding that, the anthropologists tell us there were, 12,000 years ago, only 24 million people alive on the planet. The problem is, the estimate is based on the frequency of finds of human remains from that period, which is complicated, first, by the fact that less than 1 percent of the Earth's surface has been examined for such purposes, and mainly, for second, that until those 12,000 years ago the planet was, technically, in the grip of an Ice Age, albeit receding, and most people would have lived in the warm regions of Southeast Asia, since then washed out by three major global floods, and much of it now under the sea level.

On the other hand, the aforementioned Irish legend about the first people ever to reach that country is pretty specific about the pace of the population increases.

And according to this statistical item, there should have been well over 30 million people alive on the planet some 15,000 years ago, and steeply climbing, since a Persian myth tells us 29,000 people had survived the cataclysmic termination of the Ice Age proper, some 15,500 years ago.

As we already know, though, the planet was ruined, and the population growth, realistically, would have to match the situation, and in a macabre way, it did, as most of those survivors become cannibals. In either case, by the time the critical warm-up took effect, circa 11,700 years ago, there would have been hundreds of millions of people living in Southeast Asia, most of whom would have died during the sudden warm up and accompanying global flood. On the other hand, we can also conclude that millions of people of all races would have found refuge in Siberia between 11,700 and 10,200 years ago, where fragments of their languages survive till now.

After the planet got cooled down by the asteroid impact, most of these climatic refugees started to return south, creating instant civilizations there, such as the one in Tassili, Sahara, presumably known only to the French archaeologists, as well as in India, evident from the now submerged cities.

In their new homelands the people would have started multiplying at the indicated pace, and by around 9,000 years ago the global population would have reached one billion. Yet, they were saved from the immediate consequences of that by the emptying of the immense glacial lakes, situated in Canada, into the Atlantic, likely also triggered by another asteroid impact, some 8,200 years ago.

However, this instant cooling, whose estimates range from 1°C to 5°C, lasted only about 1,000 years, after which the Earth warmed up, again suddenly, and delivered another global flood, with equally devastating consequences. This, in turn, was terminated by yet another asteroid impact, some 5,200 years ago, in the Antarctic. After this cooling the same story repeated itself.

And intriguingly enough, the Sumerian 'myth', relating the story of the latest major global flood, not only remembers, however vaguely, the time since the preceding cooling, they even knew that another flood was coming in the near future, as their strange conversation with 'gods' suggests, and built a seawall, in vain, to lessen its impact. There is even a hint of concern about overpopulation in the odd remark about the noise the city people make.

Yet, when it comes to the Sumerian rendition of the flood, the experts insist it was a riverine flood, in spite of the fact much more detailed reports, from the same time period, are available from China, describing the struggle of engineer Yü to drain the inundated low-lying regions of the country, while the Egyptians only tell us that a huge wave fell on the land. But we also know this wave terminated the pharaonic rule for about four centuries.

And whether you believe it or not, this record of human misbehaviour towards the planet goes back way further than this, as can be surmised from the 'myths' that talk about the five previous cycles of civilizations. The most detailed of these is the Seneca Indian "Legend of the Seven Worlds," or seven cycles of civilizations. Ultimately, these stories agree on one thing: They destroyed themselves by "abusing gifts of Mother Nature," and "thus disobeying Swen-i-o's wishes."

The Legend even tells us how the first three Worlds were destroyed, which enables us to date, very roughly, the time period of their existence. The first one was destroyed "by the power of the Sun," which forced the survivors to flee into the northern polar regions, as the story tells us. In turn the climatic history tells us it got so hot, circa one million years ago, that all glaciers melted. Eventually the refugees formed the Second World in the Arctic, that revived the practices of the First One. What saved the planet was the explosion of a 10 km asteroid, the astronomers call "a pile of stones," over Southeast Asia, some 800,000 years ago, which led to a whole series of ice ages. The Third World was formed close to 600,000 years ago. As the story tells us, it lasted longer than the first two combined, and was destroyed by a monster tsunami, created by the impact of yet another huge asteroid onto the continental shelf off the northwest coast of Australia, some 520,000 years ago.

The stories of the Fourth and Fifth World are literally way out of this world, to delve into at any great details here. Let it just suffice to say the Seneca Legend tells us its inhabitants realized the Milky Way is rotating. Something we did not know ourselves until about 50 years ago. Other ancient sources, including Egyptian, Mayan and Celtic, provide us with fair details of an off-planet civilization, established by the leading segment of one of the Fourth World early civilizations. The fate of the Fifth World is recorded in all the myths that speak of The War of the Gods, that took place just over 25,000 years ago, which sterilized the Earth, in the words of an Inuit myth.

It was then, thanks to the so-called sky gods, and the zoos and genetic labs they maintained aboard their cyclopean space habitats and equally big space ships, that life was gradually returned to the planet, starting some 20,000 years ago. And it is likely for this reason that, as the Seneca claim, everything revolves around the Fourth World. Ours is the Sixth World, to be terminated "by the expansion of water," which clearly predicts the global warming. The Seventh World is our final destination, where our evolution is completed.

As you, the reader, can surmise, if you have an open mind, the social evolution of mankind was not only much longer and more complex than the current scientific dogma is willing to admit, but it always was, and is, concerned with mistreatment, or an outright wholesale destruction of nature. Furthermore, if our evolution was as haphazard as the dogma claims, we would have been extinct long time ago. But we are alive, because our evolution is guided by the Cosmic Being, who is training the survivors to become the immune system of the planet, just like our immune system has to be trained.

Of course, by ignoring or denying the facts of our evolution, for the sake of a dubious dogma, we are likely exposing ourselves to greater risks than necessary, even if free will has to play its role here, in our extremely critical decision-making. The other possibility is, we simply have to derive such a decision from the knowledge we have and from our attitude towards Life at large, Life other than our own. If that is the case, consider the information you find in this slight book a mere bonus.

REALITY CHECK

Here we shall try to comprehend how things got the way they are, while focusing on different details than is the norm. Yet, we shall start with the observation that everything in this society revolves around power, and the generally accepted truism that states knowledge is power. The kind of knowledge that corresponds to this description in our world are the instrumental sciences. Ironically of its , the instrumental sciences became the king pin of all sciences, thanks to the flawed theory of evolution, totally disconnected from any hard facts. The main question is: how did it happen? On the onset of the 19th century, the German author Wolfgang von Goethe remarked: "If after 3,000 years, the civilization is unable to grasp the reigns fate, it simply has to live from day to day." And in spite the fact he had predicted, in his Faust, a mass industrialization, made possible by investment loans provided by the Devil, he never thought of the consequences of it. These started to take shape in the second half of the 19th century, when he was no longer around

The current situation began to take shape with the pan-European revolution of 1848, its core ideas encapsulated by Marx and Engels, in their *Communist Manifesto*, published the same year, that predicted the rule of the proletariat, based on historical trends. This scared the ruling British class, building their global trade empire, hence known as Imperialists, who started to look for the most effective way to repudiate this claim. They found their champion in Charles Darwin and the concept of the survival of the fittest. Yet, while featured prominently in his book "On the Origin of Species," published in 1859, the same idea was promoted by a right-wing thinker Herbert Spencer years before Darwin published his book, which then provided the needed 'scientific' backing for it. Furthermore, the evolutionary ideas found there are based on observations of domestic animals and pigeons, not on any hard evidence. That was retrofitted, decades and decades later, by the Neo-Darwinists.

Of course, the British Imperialists were a lot more concerned about the events in the real world, then the skinny *Communist Manifesto*, as its living version started to manifest itself in Germany, where the Social Democrats eventually became the largest party in the German Parliament, which led to the formation of the first welfare state in the world.

And thanks to their 99 percent literacy, apprenticeship programs and technical universities, rather limited in the UK, not to speak of its larger population and workforce, Germany started to squeeze Britain out of its export markets, and exceeded even the British mercantile shipping capacity, as well as acquired some colonies of its own in Africa.

And that was the real threat that had to be neutralized, along with Austria, its more or less identical twin. Towards that end the British Imperialists supported the Darwin's theory, as being the richest, they deemed themselves the most fit to survive, and they knew they have ascended to the lofty positions the natural way, in accordance with the Thomas Hobbes observation of nature "red in the tooth and claw."

Within years, after the book was published, Darwinism was taught at all British universities, and shortly after that at the American ones as well, with the help of the two countries rich ruling class, who understood the implications of that theory the same way.

But the British Imperialists, who felt threatened not only by the rising power of German industry and technology, but equally so by the social changes taking place in that country, were not content merely by supporting Darwinism, but decided to deal with that obstacle in a more 'natural' way. Knowing they will need allies for that, they started to spin all kinds of alliances against Germany and Austria, from the end of the 19th century, starting with the historical enemy, France, forming eventually alliances that were both overt, such as the one with Russia, and covert, such as those with Belgium and Serbia.

When ready to act, they first decided to cripple the two countries by imposing a total economic blockade; in July of 1913, with the participation of France and Belgium, which, by this act, obviously gave up its neutrality. Since that provocation did not work, the cooperative Serbian secret service arranged for the assassination of the Austrian Archduke Ferdinand in Bosnia. When even that provocation nearly fizzled out, the Serbian troops 'mistakenly' tried to cross the Danube to the Austro – Hungarian side. Yet, while these details are usually ignored, including the fact U.K. had a War Book ready, in 1914, with all the nasty details relevant to the war that started that year, while the unprepared Germans relied on decades year old plan, the rest of the sordid story is fairly well-known,

For this reason we shall now concentrate on the very flawed assumption of the monied ruling class in Britain, and ever more so in the U.S., that they can manage the affairs of this world to their advantage. And yes, it did work very well for them, for about 100 years, even if the British society did not see any substantial improvements in their living standards until the 1960s, while the American living standards surged right after World War II, mainly thanks to that war.

Of more importance though is the global situation. And, as is known by now, the current ruling class views the world exclusively through a financial prism, always on the lookout for a profit. The most obvious example would be from the volume of sales, which increase with population. In that respect, the larger the city, such as London, which grew from less than one million in 1800 to six million in 1900, as it reduced the cost of production, distribution and advertising. But the same applied to the population of the country, of the world.

Conversely, this argument was valid for the size of the companies, as large manufacturers can produce goods cheaper, and large retailers can sell more stuff. What followed, especially in the U.S., was a wave of mergers of industrial companies, formation of large department stores, and later of suburban malls, that put a lot of small retailers out of business. With such a massive push towards mega sizes, the concerns of old Malthus went out of style. Till now. At this stage, we need to turn back the pages of time a bit more, to the 16th century ideas of Francis Bacon about science.

Had the sciences abided by Bacon's dictum and established a clearinghouse of all science related ideas, not only to confirm or deny their validity, but to research their consequences, the world today would be in a lot better shape.

Probably the most crucial among these ideas was the realization of the Swedish chemist Svante Arrhenius that the Earth is getting warmer, he reached towards the end of 19th century. Of course, back then the global population was barely around 1.5 billion, and the impact of industries was fairly negligible. With these facts he calculated the Earth, with the doubling of carbon dioxide; at the rate observed during that time, would get warmer by 5°C to 6°C, albeit in 3,000 years. Of course, the IPCC would love such a projection, if still valid, but it should serve us as a warning, since it reinforces the idea that once the global population exceeded one billion, with a proportional growth of industry, the planet really started to warm up.

Decades later, Canadian born English steam engineer Guy Calendar, published, in 1938, a paper in the Quarterly Journal of the Royal Meteorological Society, trying to draw attention to the faster rise of carbon dioxide in the atmosphere, by then capable of stopping the arrival of the new ice age, expected, back then, at any time. But no one paid any heed, as the 'experts', who discussed this topic with him, deemed him to be a mere amateur.

The hints were there, but remained largely ignored, until the 1980s, when the problem was becoming all too obvious. But, again, nothing concrete was done to remedy it, and nothing concrete is being done till this day, as that would affect the corporate bottom line and the politicians' routine of milling words.

But since then, facing the literally mortal danger from the climate change, reinforced recently by a specific warning, in the journal Science, about abrupt climate warming, due to the rapidly melting methane field in the eastern section of the Siberian coast, the vast majority of societies still provide only marginal solutions, or just lip service, and we have to reflect again on von Goethe's warning, while questioning human rationality.

Yes, we are logical, but logic can be applied to a variety of conflicting subjects, ranging from ecology and economy, war and work, etc. Furthermore, as is also well known, logic has its absurd side. However, to be rational in the historical or ecological sense, requires foresight. A mental feature drastically in short supply in most people. In fact in Aeschylus' play *Prometheus Bound,* we are told quite plainly that our foresight, "Prometheus," in ancient Greek, was chained, starting some 11,700 years ago, when mankind's brains got shrunk during the tremendously hot period.

It is then the dearth of foresight that prevents us from seeing the consequences either of our action or inaction, made worse, during the last circa 150 years, by contemporary technology and plutocrats interests. With enough foresight, our entire history would have been different. And since we knew enough about the carbon dioxide's role in the climate of this planet since the 1950s, measures could have been taken to reduce the global population, and the industrial impact, by now, to a level the Earth could perhaps tolerate.

Yet, as we can see from the events of the last decade, or so, short term logic, and its related dogma, still reign supreme, accompanied by predictable screw ups, especially on the part of the Americans.

Starting with Afghanistan, where the ancient Persian sources tell us the people there were fighting each other like cats and dogs since over 3,000 years ago, and that such attitude, especially towards the outsiders, is in their genes, as proven by the subsequent history.

As far as the Middle East is concerned, it was, for centuries, a quagmire of religious, tribal, even of racial conflicts, yet the Americans stepped into it. But probably the worst example is Syria. The population there almost quadrupled, over the last 30 some years, while the global warming destroyed much of its agriculture, and hundreds of thousands of people moved to the cities, seeking jobs that were not there. When that powder keg exploded, fortified by tribal and religious differences, the West, with the U.S. in the vanguard, turned against President Assad, instead of helping him to resolve the situation, as much as possible.

At this stage, there are over 65 million refugees and displaced persons around the world, with millions of them attempting to enter Europe, where one of the countries, namely Germany, was encouraging their arrival, for perceived economic reasons. By now, there are close to 3 million refugees in the EU, with more still arriving, at this stage mainly from Africa, but meeting more and more resistance, because the politicians, again, did not foresee the consequences of their misapplied 'generosity', and because they circumvented the UN norms for seeking asylum, not to speak of the fact the UN allowed the U.S. to mess up the fragile balance in the Middle East, and joined them even in Afghanistan, where the Americans originally went to 'pacify' the country, before building a gas pipeline trough. But the bleeding heart humanitarian organizations, seeking money for the starving children in Africa, are not doing them any favor, in the long run, as in the most drought and hunger afflicted countries, such as Mali, it seems to be the norm for a woman to have a half a dozen kids, and while it is no secret that most of the people, who are bound to starve in the near future, will be in Africa, where the population is growing the fastest, while the world is running out of food and water.

The Western, especially the American and the British attitude towards Russia, also lacks rationality. Yes, of course they have annexed Crimea, but they did not invade it, as the media keep repeating, they were there, at their military and naval bases, and they did it by plebiscite, as its outcome was assured, since over 60 percent of the population are ethnic Russians. Besides, until Khrushchev 'gifted' Crimea to Ukraine, it was historically always a part of Russia. Had the West calmly accepted that as a fact of life, rather than rant about international law, that also needs to allow for specific exceptions, I am almost certain situation would have also remained calm in eastern Ukraine, which, after all, also used to be a part of Russia, and the western of the Austro-Hungarian empire. Besides, Ukraine does have the military capacity to crush that uprising, if it chose to, but for some reason opts not to use it. And now we have the case of the former Russian double agent, poisoned by a nerve gas in Britain, whose PM points her finger at Russia. Yet, the Russian inventor of this nerve gas now lives in the U.S., who, no doubt, at this stage also have the recipe for it, as does the U.K. and other countries. Furthermore, if this accusation is true, it would only prove that even the Russian intelligence services quality is slipping, which is not likely.

No doubt, Russia certainly is not, and likely will never be, a standard Western-style democracy, and neither will China, Iran or Vietnam. But it is not the Reagan's "evil empire," and even that was not crazy enough to start a war with the West. But they will stand up to anybody's bullying, as will Iran or Cuba, or North Korea.

While rationality is in short supply everywhere, it seems especially lacking in the U.S., as the people there vividly demonstrated in the last presidential election, sending a man into the White House totally unsuited for the job. But this fact not only will serve as a potent catalyst for future events, it also demonstrates how mentally sick much of the American population is, in addition to being critically desperate. To be as precise as possible, psychological tests and projections tell us that over 50 percent of the U.S. population are borderline psychotics, and 10 to 20 percent are full-blown psychotics. As such, these people can hardly be deemed rational or even logical, which also helps to explain the cascading series of screw ups and disasters at home and abroad, not to speak of the excessive violence, exploitation, and all kinds of escapism, pointing to the fact that Americans are the most alienated people in the world, but intent on remaking it in their image.

The preceding pages were but a brief outline of the flipside of our reality, but one that only relatively few people see, and the media consistently ignores. Yet now, thanks to Trump and Brexit, the gloves are coming off on both sides of the Atlantic, as the world prepares for the next stage of its evolution, largely unaware that it is coming, except, perhaps, on a subconscious level, detectable in movies about asteroid impacts, TV series, such as The Walking Dead, or even decades ago, in the book by Arthur Koestler, fittingly titled *Sleepwalkers*.

In other words, the shadow footprints of our fate were there for us, before we ever stepped into them, as we are now about to. But in spite of the fact that these footprints coincide with what some individuals realized about the human society, or glanced at specific ancient prophecies, the society, or rather its pundits, refuse to acknowledge these. And if so, not publicly.

The reason for that, again, is pretty straightforward: Events were to unfold the way they were supposed to unfold, to achieve the intended result, as they have over the last 12,000 years, to complete our evolution, in which they will succeed.

In this respect, I did not write this book to help some people to cheat on mankind's fate, but for those who can hear this voice to remember the past, and the fact that it was always the people who remembered the past who endeavoured to protect the future at any cost.

UNSTOPPABLE CHANGE

While the media tell us more people in America now believe the climate change is real, they believe in it the same way they believe in democracy, even after the latest American presidential election. They believe in it, because after years of being told about it, now more and more of them are getting pummelled by it. And while their democracy lets them do just about anything, they somehow intuit nature is kind of democratic this way too, but since they cannot shoot it, they are looking for some kind of protection from the elements that are turning as mad and violent as them.

But the same way the American pundits are unable to untie the Gordian Knot of their social problems, the climatologists are equally unable to untie the Gordian Knot of climate change, and thus, as a body, they continue to express their belief in slow gradual change that, they trust, we shall learn how to deal with, in time. If need be, with the help of hyper-expensive technology no one has the money for, that would have to be continually reapplied, without understanding the consequences. In the meantime, they keep giving us annual updates about the gases in the atmosphere, just to keep people calm.

Of course, it is not just a matter of calculating what level each atmospheric gas is going to reach, and when, as we do not really know how fast these changes will take in transforming the planet's climate. All that we do know is that melting is accelerating in both polar regions. In the Arctic twelve times faster, over the last two decades, according to the latest report on BBC. Yet, as I noted earlier, there is already enough carbon dioxide in the atmosphere that would, eventually, completely desiccate the continental US and enable trees to grow in the Arctic, with a long-time gap in between, delivering in fact a Jurassic-like climate. But no one is talking about that.

Furthermore, as the recent research by Lawrence Berkeley National Laboratory, Harvard School of Public Health, Carnegie Mellon University, and NASA demonstrates, human intellectual capacity becomes seriously impaired, especially when it comes to the use of the information strategy and crisis response, when the atmospheric carbon dioxide reaches 600 ppm. When they reach 800 ppm, these decline by 21 percent. Furthermore, these are results of short-term lab experiments only, in reality the situation likely would be a lot worse. Here I am willing to speculate that in the long-term, oversaturated with carbon dioxide, and short on oxygen, the human brain would react the same way it did during the hot spell, between 11,700 and 10,200 years ago, and become reduced even further. Perhaps by additional 20 percent, to a new average of 1,000-1,100 cubic centimetres, or to the level of Homo erectus.

But teetering on the edge of such an existential abyss, the politicians of all stripes primary concerns are economic, and while promising "sunny days," are obviously ignorant of the fact that, in addition to all the above, computerized technology would take over almost 50 percent of the current jobs, by around 2030, thus totally beggaring the vast majority of people, as there would be no funds left either for pensions or welfare, with circa 60 percent of the labour force permanently out of work. And while doing nothing about such a more defined double threat, one, again, has to wonder not only about the rationality of the politicians, but of the species at large.

In either case, at this stage, there are two scenarios vying for our attention. One is the IPCC infamous forecast for the end of the century, which envisions the global average temperature will rise, by that time, between 1.5°C to 4.5°C. This translates, even for the highest temperature, to an almost imperceptible annual increase by just 0.05°C, or next to nothing. In the meantime, the real temperature between 2015 and 2016, jumped by 0.3°C to almost 1.4°C above the pre-industrial level, or to the lowest increase predicted to take place in 85 years. Yet, as if to contradict the IPCC forecast, Scientific American predicted, in 2016, that to reach such a level, would take 10 to 15 years, while NASA and NOAA both independently predicted, in 2016, the global temperature will rise by 1°C to 1.1°C every 10 years or slightly less, without any conditional qualifying details. Projecting then this increase from 2016 to 2026, we realize the global temperature, by then, would reach 2.5°C above the pre-industrial level, but mainly it will have reached the point of runaway global warming by around 2020 or 2021.

This, in turn, is de facto confirmed by a chart, published in the May 2017 Scientific American, illustrating the expected rise of carbon dioxide emissions by 150 percent, or from two to five million tons, to be reached by 2040. Yet, now more and more bad news are coming in, concerning methane bubbling up from the thawing permafrost in the Arctic. Of even greater concern is the exponentially growing release of methane from the now melting undersea beds of frozen methane, known as clathers, along much of the Siberian coast and the northern reaches of the U.S. Atlantic and Pacific coasts.

While the U.S. clathers are located fairly deep, circa 500 m, and only about 10 percent of the methane reaches the sea surface, the rest, eaten by bacteria, that use oxygen to digest these, have the potential to warm the oceans and eventually kill oxygen producing micro-organisms. The news from Siberia is worse still. There much of the coast is a lot shallower and the clathers are melting a lot faster, releasing the methane directly into the air. In total, the Russian scientists estimate, there is at least 1,400 Gt (gigatones) of carbon locked in these clathers, of which 5 percent to 10 percent is already 'punctured' and leaking methane. Of that, they conclude, release of up to 50 Gt is highly possible at any time. And 50 Gt is 50 billion tons!

Here we have to pause and contemplate the potency of methane, as atmospheric heat agent. This usually is given as being 20 times stronger than carbon dioxide. Some claim up to 28 times more potent. If we assume a median value of 24, the 50 Gt of suddenly released methane would equal the release of 1,200 Gt of carbon dioxide, which is over 30 times more than the total global output in 2013. But where that was gradual, and 56 percent ended up being absorbed by the ocean and soil, most of this mega burp would be almost instantaneous, and head directly into the atmosphere, with unforeseeable consequences. These would include an instant rise in global temperature and more methane 'burps.' Yet, only a few short years ago, relevant 'experts' did not expect this, or similar scenario, till the 22nd century.

Furthermore, these so-called experts also seem to be in substantial disagreement about what they call GWP, or global warming potential, for methane, or for how long it remains methane, before it is transformed into carbon dioxide. I came across several references, including one in Scientific American (1.9.2012) that gave such values, ranging from 62 times to 284 times that of carbon dioxide, for the first 10 to 20 years, down to between 23 and 35 times, over 100 years, and 7 times, over 500 years. You, of course, are free to choose any of these figures, and then use it to multiply the 50 billion tons of methane with it.

The other bad news, arrived at by researchers at MIT and Simon Fraser University, thanks to their spanking new computer program that reveals the obvious: even if the world was to stop emitting carbon dioxide by 2050, atmospheric warming would continue for over 1,000 years. Something known since about 20 years ago, and grasped without computers. But then, who cares, when considering that NASA and NOAA projections that tell us the average global temperature, by 2050, would be by 5°C warmer, or reach circa 20°C, not counting the 3°C hidden, for now, by the dimming effect, consisting of pollution combined with jet trails, and our goose is bound to be roasted to a crisp.

Of course, preciously few people would survive the exodus to the Arctic, most of which would be flooded anyhow, and then they would start killing each other over the very limited sources of food there, like the caribou, seals, and polar bears, the odd fox or rabbit. But when James Lovelock broached upon such an outcome, and in a more restrained matter, some years back, in his book *The Revenge of Gaia*, he met a very negative response. But these are the facts of life, as viewed through the Neo-Darwinian prism, where evolution is an accident. But so would, oops, be our extinction, which is why the politicians and the pundits are spreading false hope, or keeping quiet. On the other hand, if that were true, mankind could not have survived all such very similar upheavals, over the ages past. Yet, we are here, and we will survive this one as well, as will the civilization this time, because we were meant to survive, since long before mankind ever existed.

And with this comes the third option, known to our ancestors since about 12,000 years ago, recorded in prophecies, often also reported in sacred texts and myths, even in Homeric stories. But the reason they were so diligently maintained was not superstition, but because they have foretold, in pretty accurate details, mankind's fate, millennium after millennium, which no human being is capable of, but only the Cosmic Being, who knew the entire future since before coming into existence, circa 14 billion years ago. And the ancient people knew that as well.

First, this ancient tradition was destroyed by the Christian Church, and in our era its validity is being denied by the official scientific establishment, as the Neo-Darwinists simply cannot imagine how would such an Entity come into existence, or how it maintains its sentience, while unwilling to except, as the quantum physicist do, the absolutely awesome computational capacity of this Entity, in comparison to which the human one is painfully puny. It is like a mayfly trying to comprehend the longevity of a whale, without ever seeing one, while also unable to comprehend how it came to be.

While the lazy anthropologists erroneously attributed to our remote ancestors the worship of multiple gods and natural forces, this actually did not start until just over 4,000 years ago, in the wake of the latest major warm-up and global flood. Before that, multiple suggestions and direct statements point to the fact people recognized only one God, the Cosmic Being, and select guardian groups, such as the Egyptian Hermetics, maintained this tradition, along with the Greek Eleusynian Mysteries, the Roman Sybils, and similar groups around the world, till Christianity put an end to it. Yet, it continued "underground," among the intellectual elite in Europe, till the late Medieval times.

But it was only Nostradamus, who had helped to rescue a key part of this ancient tradition. When on a lam from the Inquisition in Italy, he somehow came across the last section of the last nine books of the Roman Sybils, that details the upcoming events, which will terminate this civilization, to painfully usher in the final maturation of our species. And while he knew it was specifically for our age, he sprinkled in enough historical clues for people to follow his crumbs. Aside from the great fire of London he provided us with a brief outline of the American history, predicting skyscrapers, pollution and great wealth for the country, as well as the total corruption of its civil institutions. He also predicted a number of technical inventions, including the nuclear bomb, as well as the reversal of the magnetic poles, now expected by geologist as well, in the near future. Most importantly though, he also described, in great detail, the timely arrival and impact of the asteroid, also referred to by the Maya, Egyptian and Hindu sources, and quite vividly also illustrated in the section of the Bible, borrowed from Persians, titled The Revelation, but representing the returning Jesus, finally delivering the Kingdom of God.

Nostradamus tells us the asteroid will be about 1.5 km in diameter and impact near the North Pole, which the Mayas claim as well, and will do so in December, that again agrees with the ancient belief in the coming Age of Saturn, (that used to be celebrated around the middle to late December), that is expected to usher in a socio-economic transformation, from top to bottom. More importantly still, the quatrains he penned also claim this impact will trigger a new ice age, which requires at least a cursory examination.

With hints from other quatrains and predictions, we can conclude the asteroid will impact somewhere near the Svalbard (Spitzberg) Islands, forming a crater circa 30 km across, which Nostradamus named Aretusa, the ancient goddess of volcanos. Not just for the prodigious amounts of lava it will spill, along with the enormous column of debris, dust, and smoke it will eject into the atmosphere and beyond, but having likely hit a major fault line, and in conjunction with the planet quake, mentioned by Nostradamus, it will also trigger major volcanic eruptions and seismic shifts far afield.

The impact will also trigger a series of super-mega tidal waves, the first of which will be as high as the diameter of the asteroid, or about 1.5 km, when it will hit the nearest shores in Europe and Greenland, where it will rip off the vast ice fields along its eastern shores. The same mountain of water will force its way through the Bering Straits into the Pacific. Roaring south through the Atlantic, it will pulverize everything along the east coast of North America, spill into the Ohio River Valley and over the Appalachians, while simultaneously the mega tidal wave will be doing as much damage along the West Coast, until the two streams collide around the Antarctic. Yet, upon reaching the Antarctic the tsunamis still would rise some 700 m high to smash and wash out a number of the major ice fields there. This front wave will then be followed, with a much higher sea level, by at least two or three more, slightly less furious mega tidal waves, that will shatter more ice fields in the Arctic, in Greenland, and the Antarctic.

Then the immense glaciers will start quickly cooling the oceans, and this, in turn, will start cooling the warming atmosphere, triggering in the process a long series of mega storms, lashing the entire planet, shrouded for at least two years in semi darkness, by the layer of dust and soot from the impact zone, with more of the same produced by the burned forests and cities, ignited by the passing of the asteroid, by the hot ejecta from the impact zone, and likely from other volcanos.

Also, since the impact will take place so close to the North Pole, in December, northern latitudes will be the most afflicted and the moisture laden atmosphere there will start precipitating, due to the additional cold shocks, in form of snow, and likely year-round, thanks to the nonexistent summer, thus rising the albedo effect of the planet, which will aid the renewed formation of ice cover at both poles.

All of this, of course, will lead to, so far, unimagined loss of human and other life. First from the elements, hunger, and virtual absence of medical care, then from wars for survival that Nostradamus quatrains predict will start the third year after the impact.

Yet, here we should recall the mysterious drop in the content of atmospheric carbon dioxide, after World War I and the Spanish flu epidemic, that, combined, claimed about 100 million lives. Back then the loss of circa 6 percent of global population resulted in a 10 percent drop in the atmospheric carbon dioxide, with a few years delay, and a similar situation took place also after World War II, and following every asteroid impact mentioned here.

For comparison, we also need to mention the mega eruption of mount Toba, some 75,000 years ago, that ushered in a major part of the last Ice Age, a fact disputed by some climatologist, because it invalidates their precious Milankovitch theory. In either case, the volcano left behind a caldera, or crater, 30 km wide and 100 km long, or about three times the expected asteroid crater in the Arctic. But it was located only some 200 km north of the equator, and it certainly did not dislodge any glaciers, which would about equal their impact on the global climate. In the case of Mt. Toba eruption, the global surface temperature was reduced, on average, by 12°C, but by 16°C in much of North America, and likely even more inside the polar circles, where glaciers would have started to form, increasing the planets albeido, which would have led to further temperature reduction. Yet, even in this regard the expert opinions noticeably differ, which, again, invalidates their predictive ability.

From the accumulating facts, we should be able to see quite clearly that an unstoppable massive change is fast approaching, one way or the other, and it is strictly up to you to decide whether you want to believe in the uncertain, confused science of the Neo-Darwinists, and toss in the towel, or whether you believe in the life and civilization preserving act of the Cosmic Being, and decide to aid this transition to a much better world, because this transition, indeed, will need all the help it might be able to get from people who care more about the preservation of all life than about anything else.

To start with, even if NASA and NOAA forecasts were to hold out, which is not at all certain, within its first decade the Amazon forest, that absorbs circa 20 percent of Earth's carbon dioxide, would start going up in flames, and within the second decade most of North American fields would be desiccated. During the same time ice fields in the Antarctic and Greenland would start collapsing, triggering a domino effect of mega-tsunamis. These, in turn, would shatter the sea-based drilling platforms, refineries and oil storage tanks near the coasts, as well as all the ports and cities, shutting down civilization. This, in turn, would result in the release of the warming so far hidden by the dimming effect, aided by the mega-storms, triggered by the oceans, temporarily cooled down by the collapsing of ice fields. Yet, after this brief flip-flop the temperature would keep on rising, as by then there would be close to 600 ppm of carbon dioxide alone in the atmosphere, not counting other GHGs.

SCIENCE, DOGMA, KNOWLEDGE

Neither science nor technology were alien concept to our remote ancestors. We just need to put all the relevant issues into perspective. Around 15,500 years ago the last Ice Age ended in a cataclysm which only 29,000 people survived, according to a Persian myth, most of them it a subhuman state, or as cannibals, according to other Asian myths.

Yet, the Indian Tamil sources tell us of a university that survived for almost 10,000 years, while interrupted three times by global floods, the last time for good. And although the indicated periods between the floods do not correspond to the known facts, three global floods indeed devastated the planet, starting with the one around 11,700 years ago, then some 7,200 and 4,350 years ago. The other major misunderstanding is the application of the name Cankam, or Literally Academy, to such a place of learning, which the Tamils were familiar with, when it certainly was a school of ecology, as literature was of no use back then to anyone. But the learning the students acquired, as we noted, they were putting to a good use, indeed, for millennia.

While the Neo-Darwinists systematically ignore them, as they could not explain them away, the ancient sources, be they Chinese, Sumerian, Egyptian, Greek, Celtic, Inuit, Polynesian, or South American, speak of humanoid and service robots, of planes and genetic labs, of energy weapons, biological or space suits, and the Amerindians from the West Coast even of return trips across the galaxy. Of a more recent vintage are the stories about the engineer Yü, who was attempting to drain the Chinese heartland from the effects of the latest global flood, by having dykes built and canals dug, by diverting the Yellow River. Also, centuries before the Flood, engineers in Egypt and Sumer demonstrated their skills by constructing pyramids and temples, along with a sophisticated network of irrigation canals, and the Egyptians, centuries later, performed cataract operations, made dentures, used antibiotics, (in form of mold cultivated on skulls), utilized solar powered hatcheries (made out of earthenware). Later still, the engineers in Alexandria invented all kinds of mechanical contraptions, including a steam engine, used by Emperor Nero on his barque. And while in classical Athens a house-bound fly, made out of wood by Plato's grandpa, fluttered around, in Babylon two roaring mechanical lions flanked the throne, and craftsmen gold-plated objects using electric batteries. In Rome a couple of inventors produced aluminum and unbreakable glass, but wished they did not, as one of them paid for it with his life and the other had his factory demolished. The Mediaeval Europe was familiar with a mechanical eagle, and a German gunnery officer, stationed in Romania, designed plans for multistage rocket that would have flown, according to experts, using then available chemical fuels.

On the other hand, while some inventions were way too premature for a widespread use, and others just a bit, such as father Mendel's insight into genetics, when the time was right, the inventions started to pour in in multiples, sometimes being registered just hours apart at the patent offices. Furthermore, while most inventors pursue their ideas diligently, if not to say obsessively, they were often not able to come up with the right answer. At that stage, it would seem the Providence stepped in and provided one, either in a dream, while slumbering, or out for a walk, or in the form of the proverbial lightning out of a blue sky, unexpectedly. And, of course, all of these coincidences are quietly swept under the rug as well, being equally inexplicable, because to say circumstances favour prepared minds is not an explanation, in such cases.

Yet, as I noted, Nostradamus predictions for our times include not only skyscrapers and pollution, that, as we know, have definable technological origins, but also a nuclear bomb and the consequences of their use on pregnant women, as well as the space station with its arm. In other words, just like the current of history, the Cosmic Being guided the timing of our advancement of sciences and technology as well.

But it would also seem that, once this knowledge started to reach a critical level in the 19th century, we were, in a general sense, given the green light to do with these inventions as we see fit. We could say then, we are being tested, that is the scientists and engineers are, along with the politicians, and most of them are failing the test, in their willingness to collaborate in the processes that would ultimately destroy life on the planet. And if that is not evil, I do not know what is, even if it has its roots in the combination of excessive pride, vanity, avarice, ignorance, arrogance and other such human 'qualities'.

And while the scientifically minded persist in their 'Great Work', rather than dissent noisily from it, and the worst of them, the infamous Skeptics, attack and ridicule everyone who challenges their dogma of accidental universe and haphazard evolution. Consequently, even the historians and anthropologists, who, presumably studying the ancient sources should know better, acquiesce to this dogma, as do the linguists.

That, in spite of the known conclusion that most of the people on the planet spoke only one language, some 15,000 years ago. And it certainly was no crude, ultra-basic communication tool. As can be deduced from what is known about the proto-Indo-European language that descended from it, it must have been highly complex, compounded, and very flexible one, with rich grammatical features. A language that obviously had to be designed, using at least writing utensils and something to write on. And primitive, fur-wearing hunters/ gatherers do not design languages that, incidentally, have been only degenerating since then.

As one might say: So many indicators, but even more of willfully blind eyes, and it is the blind eyes and their dogma that buried, for now, any search for real knowledge, which was claimed to be the science's one and only goal. But without such search science and technology become prostitutes, tools in the hands of power-mongers, and science ceases to exist, becoming merely a desiccated branch of "study concerned with observed material facts," as it says in the dictionary. But such facts alone cannot make up science, especially since these facts are often disputable.

For all the objective reasons, original ideas in science died about 50 years ago, as was evident to some of the scientists at a conference I attended some 30 years ago. From that time, not a single original idea was put forth, but only gradual and marginal technological improvements, usually in association with computer technology, and more recently generated, or 'aided' by computers as well, along with a lot of human generated screwups. And yes, some older ideas were improved on, some flawed ideas were, perhaps, somewhat corrected, some tinkering in labs produced useful results, but that is about it.

But the devil is in the details, as the rabbis of old used to say, and so many of these details are still simply wrong.

Yet, these "details" include not only the history of our climate, but of the entire evolution of our species, all misconstrued, thanks to the ridiculous dogma. To avoid being unfair, I admit that scientists were able to figure out the likely sequence of various genetic modifications that took place over eons but they are still unable to explain the initiation and coordination of such, other than a long series of accidental but positive mutations. However, as was also calculated, if these mutations were truly accidental, no advanced life forms would exist on Earth till the Sun would go 'nova'.

While it is recognized that life, in form of amino acids, rained on Earth, which the myths know as well, the scientists are unable to say whether it was the RNA or DNA that were first formed, but mainly how, as you need DNA to create both, and how these were later modified to create ever more complex life forms. But while arguing the chicken and egg problem, they remain mum about the mystery of how such a mind-blowing sequences of four atoms ever came together, to construct future life forms. Hardly by chance. Concerning this 'dilemma', while astronomers are aware the "dark matter" is organizing the structure of the universe, some started to credit it with guiding the evolution of life on Earth as well.

The climatologists, stuck in the same dogma, keep blathering about gradual changes, and levels of atmospheric carbon dioxide, "not seen for millions of years," in spite of the fact all the past catastrophic warm-ups are making such pronouncements ridiculous.

But this dogma gets its greatest jollies with the human evolution. While indulging in the "out of Africa" nonsense, along with the story of obviously regressed Neanderthals, it completely ignores the story of Homo antecessor, most likely indigenous to Europe, whose presence there is in evidence from circa 1.3 million to 800,000 years ago, virtually identical to us, according to the Scientific American. At first, their cranial capacity, based on a sole find of a partial child's cranium, was given as 1,000 cc, but more finds led to its expansion of up to 1,400 cc, matching that of the de facto same species, known as Homo heidelbergensis, who existed on the same continent from 800,000 to 300,000 years ago, that also had a cranial capacity ranging from 1,000 to 1,400 cc. Homo sapiens likely are but a continuation of the same species from 300,000 years ago, especially since their presence in North Africa and the Middle East was recently moved up from 200,000 years ago to 300, 000 years ago. Yet, this standard classification omits the Cro-Magnons, with cranial capacity ranging from 1,450 to 1,800 cc, who were around between 45,000 and 12,000 years ago, as that 'disturbs' their 'theory'.

And only recently the 'scientists' started acknowledging the human cranium got shrunk, but are unable to say when or why, never mentioning it was a form of regression. Yet then, since about 6,000 years ago, the shape of our skulls started to change, from long and narrow, to round with a bulging forehead, the seat of imagination and future related tasks. This transformation then really took off during the Little Ice Age. Again, the Neo-Darwinists offer no explanation of the cause of this transformation. Furthermore, even the Peking Man, who the Chinese claim is their ancestor, had a forerunner in the Nihewan Man, who lived in China as far back as 1,350,000 years ago, according to the November 1991 article in the journal Nature.

Also, while acknowledging we have evolved from a walking ape, the experts always talk about Lucy, who walked the Earth some 3.5 million years ago, but never about the species of a walking ape known as Dryopithecus fontani, indigenous to Europe, some 18 million years ago. At the same time, there are indications, ranging from a 14 million-year-old boot print, found in the southwest U.S., to the global stories of an ancient human race now living underground, along with the fact that millions of years of data are missing from that period, we shall be content here with suggesting that some of these walking apes walked all the way to Africa, and for some reason remained apes.

Sadly, by now science not only ceased to seek objective knowledge, but most of it, serving the technological juggernaut, turned into a baited dead end that would soon decimate mankind from within and without, by denying us self-knowledge, that is the real facts of our evolution, of the meaning of life and history. Worse yet, by undermining our imagination, will, IQ and self-reliance with a glut of superficial 'info', cheap TV thrills and electronic toys, while promising ever more of the same in the future, with electronic implants and genetic modifications. Yet, that, in turn, would also destroy the little creativity we have left, along with our humanity, preventing us from ever finding a way out of this trap. And that is no improvement, but sheer evil.

Of course, we need knowledge, but one that would open our eyes and minds to the greater interconnected reality, instead of shutting us in details of isolated facts, connected only by their presumably accidental origin and nature. This sort of 'philosophy' only serves those who want to dominate mankind, to make it do their bidding, which is why their lackeys shout to the world that only their way of interpreting reality is valid and all others are heretics and heathens. But even as a boy, once I lost the induced fear of hell, invented by the Church, I realized I would rather end up in hell, with all the bright, open minded people, than forever sing hallelujah with the fearful, dull-minded angels. Now I feel the same way about this civilization and its science. And perhaps not so surprisingly, more and more people do, with the prospects becoming ever clearer and more dangerous.

But while such dissenting voices are still rather rare, one can find useful bits and pieces of knowledge, not 'info', scattered by the body of science, almost by omission. One only needs to know, from the established context, whether they ring true or not. Some of the scientist, while reeling off the lines of their scientific catechism, occasionally insert a genuinely interesting item or two, if one can catch it and insert it where needed.

There are also other sources as well, most of them a bit dated for modern readers, especially of the youngest generation. I am, of course, referring to the myths, sacred texts, even classical fairy tales, books about Medieval alchemy and learning, Greek sources, Roman historians or Aeschylus plays. Admittedly, much of the stuff is rather boring, unless you are stubborn about "doing your thing." At least they taught me a measure of patience.

But to save you the time, I am providing the gist of what I have learned here, and in the other books I wrote, while always trying to tell the truth. Not the way I want to see it, but the way it objectively is, because objectivity is the main tool in such a search, and only objectivity can establish a decent level of trust between someone like me, promoting unorthodox ideas, and the readers. And if you do not believe, check out the sources I used and decide for yourself.

BELIEVE IT OR NOT

As already noted, the human brains shrunk, by some 20 percent, during the heat spike between 11,700 and 10,200 years ago. While some anthropologists finally started to recognize the fact, without admitting it abolishes their theory of evolution, they seem unable to agree on the timing and the cause. I deduced mine from the emergence of matriarchy and reference in a South American myth claiming that men, in comparison to women, became mentally like animals, but mainly from the shock and horror expressed in many myths, in which people describe themselves as asleep, or as living dead, in the aftermath of this transition, which was the beginning of our historical period. And if anyone paid attention to such things, it was also noticed that, even currently, boys and young men are intellectually slipping more and more behind girls and young women, as the climate warms up. This is noticeable also in the fact more female students graduate from universities than male students.

We can also take que from the German team of archaeologists, who excavated, what was termed a "temple complex," in Gobekli Teppe, Turkey, constructed, they concluded, between 12,000 and 10,000 years ago, and duly noted the declining level of creativity during its construction.

What is really peculiar though, is that right alongside the stories expressing their horror at such a critical mental step down, we also have stories that promise this step down will be fully reversed some 12,000 years from the time it took place, or about now, which also helps to date this event.

Yet, it is only through such "promissory stories," by some hints in the Bible, in the Mayan *Popol Vuh*, and in the Aeschylus play *Prometheus Bound*, that we can, up to a point, try to visualize what actually the human species lost in the step down. But before we can do that, we have to discuss, however briefly, the true nature of reality of this world.

The mainstream scientific dogma of our times, driven by the materialistic sciences, promoted by the self-styled Skeptics, insists that the universe and the life within it emerged and evolved by accident. Then there is the other school of thought that includes microbiologist and astronomers, led by quantum physicists. The last group realized that the material universe, 'constructed' out of quantum particles, as well as the life within it, had to, repeatedly, overcome mathematical impossibilities, to become what they are. And having eventually calculated the computational capacity of the newly emerged universe, they realized that, in order to achieve the seemingly impossible, it had to have known the entire future even before it emerged, and started calling this Entity the Cosmic Being.

Of course, since quantum particles make up everything there is, the Cosmic Being is everywhere and everything, however incomprehensible that might seem to us, and the ancient people knew that too, as the Egyptian Hermetics spelled it out for us, referring to the Cosmic Being as Atum: "To conceive of Atum is difficult. Define him is impossible … He is bodiless, yet embodied in everything … Throughout the cosmos he disseminates life and movement. Atum works with nature, within the laws of necessity, causing extinction and renewal …"

However, the Hermetic texts also contain prophecies that they deemed relevant, such as this one: "In times to come, clever intellectuals will mislead the mind of man …" which, I am quite certain, refers more to the present than, perhaps, to Christianity and other modern religions. More importantly still, referring to mankind's role in a fairly near future, the texts have this to say: "The Earth is kept in order by means of humanities knowledge and application of the arts of sciences, for Atum willed that the world should not be complete until man had played his part." And from this we can surmise the completion will arrive with mankind becoming Earth's immune system.

At this stage, try to keep the above in mind, because we need to backtrack here a bit.

As the historians know, most of the ancient people believed this God was also guiding the fate of the nations, and worried about the outcome of every major battle, in spite the fact a single battle or war can't have such an effect. However, one of the texts recorded in Egypt, some 5,000 years ago, no doubt from a much older source, provides us with a very rough outline of events from the last 12,000 years, which agree with the little that we do know about it. There are also the Nostradamus' prophecies, whose origin, via the so-called Roman Sybils, goes back to the same ancient source. The most convincing part of it, that makes both predictions relevant, is the brief outline of key events in the future United States, made likely millennia before any human had a notion there would be such a place. Furthermore, all these predictions, up to the total corruption of all American institutions, had been perfectly fulfilled. But for the predictions to be fulfilled, history had to unfold exactly the way it did, and no other, as the readers of science fictions will know.

And it did, leaving for us the fingerprints of how it was done. I did my homework on this subject as well and present here the key examples of that.

The first two concern ancient Greece and its role in securing Europe for the historical role it eventually played in the fate of this world.

The very first series of events, or rather sea battles, involves Persia, the major power in the region, and of its Carthagenian allies. They, especially the Persians, brought hundreds of ships to the conflict, against a much smaller Greek force. But in three separate storms most of the Persian ships were destroyed and the Carthagenians, heading for Sicily, lost all the ships with horses and chariots. The Greeks were the obvious victors.

The second series of events is all about Alexander the Great and his conquest, that really secured Europe's safety until the time of the Roman Empire.

The third series of events is about three subsequent Spanish Armadas, sent to conquer England, with all three scattered and wrecked by storms, for which the English thanked the divine intervention. Without it North America would speak Spanish, the prediction about the United States would have remained unfulfilled, and science and technology, under the watchful eye of the Church, which was trying to ban steam locomotives in the 19th century, certainly would not be what they are today.

The fourth example is a singular, almost innocuous event, that took place at the opening stage of the battle of Midway. Of all the Japanese scout planes sent out, only one spotted the American aircraft carriers. But his radio failed and he was unable to relay their location. In view of the Japanese advantage in the number of carriers and planes, and of a surprise, it is highly likely that the Japanese would have won the battle, if only the darn radio worked, and then who knows how the war would have turned out in the Pacific, throughout Asia and in China, perhaps even in Europe.

And now again back to the place where we took the illustrative detour. Namely to the promise of restoring mankind's mental capacity and what that might entail.

Knowing what we do about the climate, we realize that mankind had, for most of the times, evolved under the ice age conditions. Even the craniums of the very first fully human beings, Homo antecessor, who were around for hundreds of thousands of years, on both sides of the one million years ago timeline, ranged from 1,000 to 1,400 cc, with the larger brains either prior to one million years mark, when it got hellishly hot, thanks to their activities, or closer to our times, perhaps during an ice age period.

That also means large brains, by themselves, are not necessarily the result of evolution, but what is inside of them, how they, namely their priorities, are structured internally. But the structure of the brain in turn is reflected in the organization of the society, and that, in fact, our evolution was all about, as something our ancestors were aware of. In one of the African myths it is referred to as "ongoing creations." The Egyptians jesters used to refer to the current cycle of it as a ball of dung, in which the scarab beetle, who represented evolution, is rolling the next generation(s). And the Seneca Indians tradition claims ours is the last era before mankind evolution is completed.

And, as far as I know, only two sources speak rather explicitly about what people will be experiencing when they reach that stage. The Bible states that men and women will again be able to prophecy. At the same time, it also tells us only the God knows the future, which would imply at least one way communication from the God, for the people to know the future. Nostradamus, on the other hand, is a lot more explicit, and he tells us people will be able to perceive the world through the mind of the Almighty. Interpreting this with the Maya record of the ability their ancestors used to have, before losing it, we could say that people will be able to perceive the world both on a micro and macro level, as well as its future, and to heal themselves.

Yes, there is still a third source, the Aeschylus' *Prometheus Bound*, in which the playwright tells us how Prometheus, who represents mankind's "foresight," or rather "foreknowledge," was bound, and is to be released in 12,000 years. The same span of time is indicated by Persians, Egyptians, and by the Indian cycle of Meha Yuga.

The question twitching on the tip of most peoples' tongues likely would be: But how? How could the quantum Cosmic Being, who is the only Entity that knows the future, communicate with people? And the answer to that question is built right into every living cell, especially those inside our brains, for each cell's structure is supported by the microtubules, which not only perform the role of a transport system, but, above all, act as a quantum computer, coordinating all the cell's thousands of concurrent functions, and likely are also involved in the evolutionary changes. However, to receive such a communication, a critical level of such receptors is probably required, but with the smaller brains, we have lost that capacity. And since the brain can expand only during ice age conditions, the prophecies, retained for us in Egypt, in the Bible, and via Nostradamus by the Roman Sybils, all promise the return of an ice age, courtesy of another asteroid impact, altogether at least fourth such major climate altering impact, since those 10,200 years ago. The key difference will be in timing, as this impact will take place before the major warm-up will take effect, because, by then, it would be rather too late and only exacerbate the destruction, as it would decimate the survivors who will have fled to the northern polar regions, if arriving even a few decades from now.

This fact too was known, and it was recorded for us by clergyman Johann Friede (1204-1257): "When the great time will come, in which mankind will face its last, hard trial, it will be foreshadowed by striking changes in nature. Not all of it will be the result of natural causes [as] mankind will gamble with its own existence. Before the powers of destruction will succeed, the universe will be thrown in disorder and the Age of Iron will plunge into nothingness."

These are hardly coincidental ideas, that would have popped up in peoples' minds, vastly separated in time and place, but arrived at via the underground river of knowledge, released some 12,000 years ago, when people still had the capacity to receive this from the Cosmic Being, and deemed it of such a crucial importance to all of mankind, people endeavoured to maintain it for millennia. Yet, even the demise of this information was predicted, and we can thank for this the Church and the current scientific dogma.

But peculiarly enough, while Nostradamus' collection of relevant prophecies remains silent about the causes of the coming upheavals, in the Bible the sentence "God will destroy those who destroy Earth" is being repeated in several sections. And while it is admitted even in the Bible that God created evil [Isaiah 45–7], it would likely be better to say the Almighty allows the evil to take place, to make us choose, to shape our minds. After all, even the Almighty's choice is limited by natural laws, which the Hermetics also knew, calling them "the laws of necessity."

Hence also the question of free will, which some of the Sceptics are attempting to deny, and which question can also sneak into the minds of some of those who read or hear that the Cosmic Being knows the entire future, and that the future is thus determined.

And, indeed, the specific bifurcation points are obviously determined, but their required direction is finalized by a few individuals, whom the ancient Greeks called "heroes," as they had no will of their own, so to say, but carried out the will of the gods. And these individuals, indeed, come in good, evil, even 'neutral' varieties, such as Roosevelt, Hitler or Alexander the Great. The rest of us, mere mortals, have to decide which, if any, of these "heroes" we want to follow.

What might be still less believable, is that the Bible also contains passages that echo the preceding pages, or compliment them even further. And the most striking example is the stunning and never publicly discussed admission, found in Isaiah 43/10, where the Lord says, "Before me there was no God formed, neither shall there be after me." This description, beyond any doubt defines the Cosmic Being, and most likely was borrowed from an Egyptian, Persian or Ethiopian source. The concept of God as the Universe is further confirmed in Acts 17/28: "For in him we live and move, and have our being."

Another odd remark, without any relevant context, is found in the Revelation 17/10: "And there are seven Kings: Five are fallen, one is, and one is to come yet." Like most people, I would have ignored this senseless sentence, had I not remembered the Seneca Indian Legend of the Seven Worlds, in which the concept of Worlds the ignorant Beduins reduced to 'kings'.

Without any definable connection to the source of the catastrophic reduction of the human cranium, the references to it, abounding in the Eastern Mediterranean, viewing it as a state of sleep or living death, found its way into the Bible as well: "For the Lord hath poured out upon you the spirit of deep sleep and upon the prophets and your rulers," (Isiah 29/10), and in the Revelation 1/5: "Jesus Christ, the first begotten of the dead."

On the other hand, the reversal of our mental slump is represented in the Bible, preceded, as if it were, by warning: "And there shall be a Great Tribulation. And except those days should be shortened there should be no flesh saved …"

(Matthew 24/21-22). This is then balanced by a promise from the God: "... Afterwards I will pour out my spirit upon all flesh and your sons and daughters shall prophecy." (Joel 2/28) I.e. know the future, again.

The key event itself, the asteroid impact, is described in great and confused detail in The Revelation as "... a great mountain burning with fire was cast into the sea and there arose a smoke out of the pit and the Sun and the air were darkened ... by the smoke ..." (8/8 and 9/2).

Yet, we also need to keep in mind that this event is to fulfill a two-fold purpose: It represents the second coming of Christ, this time as an asteroid, delivering the kingdom of God. The Bible is also quite clear about the consequences. In Isaiah 14/20 - 21 we can read this: "The seed of evildoers ... who destroyed the land shall never be renowned." This last word though can be read either as "their inheritance will be infamy," or depending on the original translation "shall never be renewed," while The Revelation revels in condemnation of merchants, or business people, and predicts their demise, as does the Greek Iliad and Nostradamus. And interestingly enough, in Isaiah 32/15 we find this rather important statement: "Until the spirit is poured upon us from high and the wilderness be a fruitful field and the fruitful field be counted for a forest." This clearly indicates the future transition to an ecological society.

And finally, returning to The Revelation (21/22) we find that "there will be no temple" in the City of God and that "the mystery of God should be finished." Curiously enough, we are also told that while this City is all gold, but "invisible as glass." Yet, in Isaiah 1/26 it is the people who live there who are compared to the "city of righteousness." Thus, amidst all the pompous blather and dubious symbology, hiding the absence of understanding, we are told that in this new golden age era people will need no temples, as with their new understanding they will perceive of this God everywhere and deem it, the entire universe, as the Temple of this God, with whom they will be able to communicate. And there is no need to add anything to this.

CIVILIZATION AND ITS NATURE

The dictionary defines civilization as a society with advanced arts and sciences, with corresponding social, political and cultural complexity.

This contemporary definition would in turn require careful definition of its individual components, starting with the word "advanced," because the contemporary arts, in general, are anything but advanced. The sciences, of course, are more advanced than they were in the 19th century, but if science was to define our understanding of the world, we are only at a confused starting point. And even the word "complexity" should be replaced with confusion or chaos, especially when it comes to the American civilization.

Yet, civilization has been around for millennia. The very first one, in our era, was situated in Tassilli, today's Sahara, and its urban areas, connected by roads, featured arenas with parking lots for chariots. This existed roughly between 10,000 and 8,000 years ago, when the region was green and fertile. The next, equally unknown civilization, that constructed a cluster of huge pyramids in today's Bosnia, was likely created by the descendants of the Tassilli people, the ancestors of the Europeans. And even when these started to migrate, slowly, into the heart of Europe, about 7,000 years ago, forced by the warming climate, these people had a civilization, as evident from the remains of their urban settlements and temples, all written about by the archaeologist Marija Gimbutas in her books.

After all, the best definition of a civilization likely would focus on the ability of the society to organize for survival of ecological disasters and climatic swings, which most of the early societies, be they European, Sumerian, Chinese and Egyptian clearly demonstrate. Furthermore, their religion and the arts associated with it, filled with meaning and transcendent symbolism, point in the direction of the Cosmic God. But then, the Medieval art often displayed the same quality. Modern art, by and large, is but an expression of personal neurosis, or of striving for financial success.

Considering the above evaluation of the term, our civilization represents a mixed bag of the qualities assigned to it. While our science is definitely more advanced than it, historically, ever was, it also ended up being hogtied by the dogma of its own making, and is no longer pursuing objective knowledge, wherever it may lead. The 'arts' though, in general, are regressing into primitivism, which can hardly be called "complex," as it consists, with very rare exceptions, only of surface, being hollow. And while Canada, some of the European countries and China are, for now, managing the ever-growing complexity of problems, there are signs that these compounding problems would soon swamp them as well, and the world would follow the fate of all the preceding historical civilizations.

But this civilization is blatantly failing when it comes to the most basic definition of it, as an instrumental organization for survival. This is not only in evidence now, but was, since over 50 years ago, when the climatologists, in compliance with their theory, at the time, were expecting the "return" of the ice age, yet nowhere were there any signs of preparations for that. On the other hand, according to the Milankovitch's theory, the ice age should have arrived 2,000 years ago, when it got so balmy, the sea level rose by 1,5 meter.

In the meantime, as noted by some current observers, mankind became its sole purpose and end, almost devoid of any connection to nature and its vagaries, simply because the climate was, all in all, stable, for the last circa 150 years. This gave some people the idiotic notion we can dominate it and do on the planet as we please – in part thanks to our relative advances in science. The problem is, this science is concentrating on earning huge profits for corporations, instead of securing our survival, as it should, by examining all the details that could have any bearing on it. In this respect we can also say that, if our science is advanced, it is advanced in the wrong direction, not in the one that would benefit the society. If it were, the sciences, as a body, would have focused a lot more on nature and its needs, and favour the life-sciences over math and physics, computers and the computer driven technology.

This shift, that likely started during World War I, with the development of new technologies for the war, then continued in the same direction ever since, drawing ever further from life sciences and the study of nature, also because mastering the knowledge of technology is a lot easier than mastering the knowledge of nature, and it pays better.

But it is also thanks to this shift, and the general neglect of everything associated with nature, we are now finding ourselves up the smelly creek, with the world grotesquely overpopulated, and on the brink of self-destruction. And in that sense the old struggle between culture and nature is reaching a new dimension, as the culture, represented by the megacities, is now in the final stages of obliterating what is left of nature in most parts of the world.

At the same time, we need to note that, at this stage, 52 percent of the global population lives in cities and megacities and 82 percent in urban areas. The conditions in these agglomerates then led to what is termed "a new tribalism," by creating a hostile environment, in many respects similar, mentally, to hot or cold deserts, or dense jungles, where isolation makes it impossible to maintain, much less to create, a high civilization.

And that is also where the roots of many internal human conflicts lie, for most of our evolution we have lived in contact with nature, we were shaped by this proximity, both mentally and physically. Now most of the people are treading on an alien ground that is warping their humanity. And no one says anything, no one does anything about the situation, even in the so-called 'developed countries', in spite of knowing the following: 1. Human DNA can change due to circumstances. 2. Also due to the environment and culture. 3. And the kind of surroundings characterizing people's domicile.

In the anthropological sense, "culture" refers to the sum of values acknowledged by the respective societies, listed under the preceding items 2. and 3., and as we know, by now, human culture tends to be self-destructive, as demonstrated by the five preceding cycles of it. Plus, obviously, thinking of the next culture, its members will need to ensure their civilization is made up of somewhat different components, and that they will need to define the quality of these components beforehand.

Concerning the social, political and "cultural" values, these will need to address the core needs of a typical society, such as survival and the level of cooperation, yet remain simple, in order for the society to act in a complex way, unlike in the present, where the reverse is true. The same would apply to science, and even more so to the technology derived from it. The concept of art will have to be very carefully defined to ensure it expresses and reinforces the society's key values, in a sophisticated multi-level way, as expected from a true art.

In today's terms, cacophonic noise or hurdy-gurdy is not music, splatter of paint or pussycat is not an art, doggerels or snippets of mundane reality are not poetry, musicals or plays dissecting social or psychological problems do not belong on stage, books written by hacks, academicians for credit, or published for assured economic success, are not worth the paper they are printed on. For music to be music, it has to contain elements of melody and some rhythm, and anything written has to contain well expressed ideas and imagination, without distorting reality. And since both also need to be uplifting, they must never pander to the lowest common denominator.

As far as nature is concerned, I think I have said enough about it to make it obvious that close proximity to it influences all people in a positive way, especially when experienced as a part of one's inner being.

ANIMALS AND TREES I KNEW

My boyhood encounters with animals did not turn out all that well, for the animals. The crayfish died in a bidet, where I tried to cook it, believing it would turn red. It did not. The leech escaped from the jar, but desiccated on the central heating. The hedgehog, by incessantly trying to climb out of the pail, kept my parents up, and I was ordered to take it where I found it – along with all the bugs infesting it. But on the street, as kids, we snuggled up to the postal and beer delivery horses, feeding them apples and carrots, when these were available. Also, a couple of classmates kept hordes of white mice between the double windows, using them probably for insulation in winter, or who knows what they were doing with them. One such white mouse bit me, after I cornered it on the hospital grounds, nearby, which made the lab people panic, thinking it might have escaped them, infected with something dangerous. But once I started spending summers on the farm of the people my parents befriended, my animal horizon vastly expanded, as there were cows, a big horse named Carl, a bull, for communal insemination, as well as a pair of breeding pigs, hens, of course, as well as a miserable mole killing cat.

Not having much else to do with my time there, my morning and afternoon 'chores' consisted of tagging along, when the farm boys were taking the cows to pasture, where, one day, I discovered that by grabbing a cow by the tail I can go "grass skiing," as the animal lurched and ran. Then, early in the evening, I crawled all over the barns, looking for the eggs the hens hid there. But almost every year one of them delivered a surprise, in form of a brood of tiny chicks.

And talking of parenting instincts, once only the people there had a little mongrel dog, and he fathered pups with a mongrel bitch from the farm just up the hill. Peculiarly, this little doggie father ran up the hill, every day, always around 1:00 pm, to visit with his family.

But the most memorable events there concerned the large animals. The horse, Carl, the nameless bull, and a pair of horses from another farm in the village, where I made myself at home.

A part of my unspoken contract was to unharness Carl every time he was done with his chores. I did my job as usual that day, but instead of walking placidly into his stable, this big animal spun on his hind legs like a ballet dancer and dashed across the yard for the gate to the orchard, half of which was wide open. And just as he was to bolt through it, my mom appeared there. Carl's hooves dug into the ground and his forward motion momentarily froze. My mom ducked behind the closed portion of the gate, and Carl resumed his gallop.

The incident with the two horses was just a different version of the animal altruism towards humans. It was during the final leg of the trip, with the horses pulling a huge load of hay up a steep hill, with me sitting atop one of them. Because of the steep incline, my inexperience, and the lurching motion of the horses, I slipped off and fell between the two horses. They too immediately froze in their forward movement, half of their hooves up, to avoid stepping on me, with their bulging eyes staring down at me. I just rolled out between the legs of the horse on the right, to the edge of the road, and they resumed pulling the hay wagon.

The event with the bull represents to me a fleeting moment of freedom for this animal, who only was taken out of the stable to impregnate someone's cow. One day, Thomas, the young farmer, decided on a lark to hitch up the bull to the hay wagon, and a whole gang of us went along. We piled this four metres long wagon with over two metres of hay and clambered to the top. Everything went fine, until we got to a narrow field road, build-up of stones to a height of about one metre, on the downslope. And that is where the bull got his fit of freedom and started to run, for the joy of it, disregarding the pain in his nose, caused by the steel ring there, at which Thomas was yanking, trying to make him stop, while the rest of us were deciding whether to jump, or looking where we might land, if, or when, the wagon was to topple over the edge of the road. But we all made it safely back to the farm, where the bull stopped in front of his section of the stable he shared with Carl.

In Canada, my notable experiences with domestic animals were limited to two country dogs, I ran into on private properties, but fortunately for me, well-trained. The third one, being a puppy, was not trained at all. It found a home at a house of a poor printer in Toronto, where I used to bring him extra treats and took him out for walks. Then, after almost two years of absence I came by again, and the now grown-up dog came running, wiggling like a little puppy. That made me think of the 'scientific research' into the extent of dogs' memory and of the scientists' power of observation, or the lack of it.

In and near Toronto, I also made interesting observations of 'lowly' insects and birds. The most interesting one involved a green grasshopper, who jumped onto my brown cord pants, while I was reclining on a meadow outside the city. I tickled its bum and it jumped off. To my surprise though, it was back, within a minute, performed another symbolic nibble, looked at me and jumped off again. And yes, scientists talk with disdain about the amateurish anthropomorphism, but to me it still represents a clear sign of an inter-species communication, or the grasshopper's "thank you for not hurting me," performed at such a risk.

The other accidental insect encounter was a wrestling match between two ants, they engaged in, using their hind legs, on a sidewalk, which they continued with in spite of my nosey presence. When done, they just walked away in opposite directions.

The other memorable incident from Toronto concerns two groups of starlings I encountered at the opposite end of the same street, near Bloor and Dufferin. First, I noticed a flock of starlings descended on a grassed patch there, to feed on the bugs and grub. But after the lot of them took off, two or three cheats returned to vacuum the patch. Then, another surprise, in form of three or four starling 'cops', who appeared out of nowhere, to confront the crooks. These, after a very brief standoff, followed the departed flock.

In Spain I encountered ants practising burials. Noticing the fact, I sacrificed one unfortunate ant, and placed the body near the mound. The ordinary workers seemingly ignored the body, until an undertaker ant emerged from within the mound, where all the other bodies came from, as far as I could tell. This ant picked up the body and carried it quite a distance, to the concrete steps leading down to a stream. There, at the bottom of perhaps the third step from the top was a sizeable crack, inside of which presumably was a large cavity, where this, and the other such ants, were depositing the bodies of their fellows.

In Mexico I saw large golden coloured ants, whose uniqueness was just their colour, as I never saw or heard of such ants before or after. I also saw there a tiny wee snake, by the side of the road, about the size of an earthworm, but perfectly shaped reptilian head, with two black dots for eyes. When I stooped down to look at it, it raised its tiny head and looked me in the eyes, as if asking the obvious question: what's your intention, big thing? All I did was to marvel at its existence, as it was so obviously unfit for survival. Yet, there it was, in all its miniscule glory.

I became acquainted with nature, namely the things that grow out of the ground, like trees, by the time of my third birthday, courtesy of American bombers, who unloaded their deadly cargo over Prague, totally ignorant of the fact it was an occupied capital of their ally. One bomb hit the building my parents lived in, and exploded in the basement, killing all the people there, and the other bomb exploded on the street, shattering the apartment. My mom and I have survived by sheer luck, walking at the time through the entrance passageway. Afterwards, for about a year, we lived in a village, outside the city, where my relation to such growing things started to bud, without knowing it.

The apartment in Prague we then moved into, faced the garden of a Franciscan monastery, where the monks sometimes played football. But wedged into their property was a small park, with a lot of lilac bushes and a variety of trees, on its steep slope. These also included several trees with reddish bark, producing an abundance of pink flowers every spring. Eventually, I found out these were the sakura trees from Japan, which led to my early, and brief fascination with Japan, mainly its aesthetics, as they're also hung on the apartment walls a couple of Japanese prints, left there by the previous German tenants.

Also, within about two blocks from the apartment were three public parks and a botanical garden. On the top of that, my parents always brought me along for their weekend hikes, which, being rather young, I often completed by viewing the countryside from the perch on my father's shoulders. And by the time I was six, I was dispatched, with my grandpa, to enjoy nature, and he diligently dragged me out, almost every morning at 5:00 am, to pick mushrooms in the forest. About a year or two later my parents started to rent chalets, in the summer and winter, on the slopes of the mountains in northern Bohemia.

But my intimate relationship to nature did not really start taking shape until we started spending summers on the aforementioned farm in southern Bohemia, especially from my teens, when my parents built a small cottage on the ridge above the village, with a spectacular view of forests, fields, villages, and mountain ranges rolling beyond the horizon, and grazing deer outside the window early in the morning. It was most likely there I came to associate nature with peace and quiet, as the road was distant and the traffic sparse, the greatest 'noise' nature there produced, was the bubbling brook in the forest, or its trees rustling in a wind.

I enticed the first girlfriend I brought there to go hiking in the ancient forest preserve, covering the mountain we could see from the top of the ridge, in the opposite direction. But to get there, we had to take a bus and a train, and then walk a lot further than I imagined. The scenery was spectacular though, with so many centuries old trees all around, and not a single human being. This fact shortly explained itself, as it rather suddenly got dark, and not a hint of civilization in sight, until we stumbled upon a solitary hayloft on stilts, put there by the foresters. And that is where we slept, to be woken up in the middle of the night by a boar, rooting for something underneath.

After I left the old country, I did not really commune with a forest until years later, in Ontario, and New York State. The greatest disappointment was the almost impenetrable bush, north of Toronto, in places practically 'paved' with moraine, and my dissatisfaction with that fact in turn ticked off the young lady I was there with. But I visited the planted, open forests, in southern Ontario, more than once. On the other hand, the Adirondack National Park, while majestic, the view of it, from a tower, rather freaked me out, stretching, unbroken, from horizon to horizon. At least my emotional response to it was appreciated, making the rounds of Toronto poetry workshops, I was told.

But the less I was able to enjoy them, by browsing through them, the more I read about them and their historical role, the more I thought and was concerned about their fate. After all, it has been known for decades trees communicate with each other via electro-chemical signals between their roots, which is not dissimilar to the way the human brain works. They even have a rather similar structure to neurons as well. This not only suggests (proven) awareness, but also a form of consciousness. When I presented the idea to a forest biologist, he first argued against it, then agreed. But now this fact is elaborated on, with many more beautiful details, in a book *The Hidden Life of Trees* by German forester Peter Wohlleben.

My nagging feeling, that I am attempting to impart here, is that the entire nature, not just us, but animals, birds, fish, trees, everything that is alive, one way or the other, possesses a form of consciousness and intelligence, even of sentience, as was recently suggested about fish. And experiments demonstrated vegetables and flowers can detect our negative intentions, like yanking them out of the soil, and 'scream' in terror. The irony is, the scientific dogma was preventing us from grasping, till now, that all these animals and other life forms, have been evolving for a lot longer than we have, and in a sense, are more perfect than us, at this stage, for the role they play in life, suitable for their situation. Yet, because of our ignorance, we keep treating nature as a mere 'resource', and now we risk a total destruction of it.

What helps me to retain mental balance, and prevents me from deceiving myself into false optimism, is the realization that the generally accepted concept of reality, provided by the current science, is deeply flawed. Of course, we have reasons to be greatly concerned and worried, but mainly about where we stand in our attitude towards life, not whether mankind or civilization will survive the coming upheavals.

Let us consider this as an example. Reflecting on the potential fate of the Amazon Forest, I realized that during the Ice Age that place, being almost on the equator, was a dry savannah. A question came to my mind: where did the rich variety of life there come from, that it is today known for? As far as I know, no one had either asked nor answered this question.

And while reflecting on the balmy idea some scientists expressed, namely that mankind is to become the planet's brain, at this stage of our evolution, let us also consider the possibility it was once the global forest that was the planet's brain, regulating its temperature, it's water cycle, and thus the ability for all life to survive. Yet, it was the 'brains' of this mankind that have been systematically killing it, for millennia, and now we are about to finish this job.

In fact, if anything, mankind's fate, one way or the other, is to become arborists, or to perish. In a larger context, of course, we are meant to become the planet's immune system, as mentioned earlier. This, to a greater extent, will mean protecting the re-expanded global forest from fires, by keeping the forest ground free of any combustible debris, while ensuring it is covered in grass and moss, and with enough ponds there to water the animals, or to put out a fire. Having taken care of the local problems, emergency crews would need to act swiftly, if the forested regions would be impacted by asteroids, or ignited by lightening.

At the same time, our attitude towards all the non-human life will have to change as well, and never ever use them as a 'resource', because their population, outside of the human domains, always sustainable in size, will be controlled naturally, by homeostasis. Within the human domains, the semi-wild population of animals, residing in the forests there, will be controlled, seasonally, by culling, as will be the excess population of young males among the domestic animals, while the rest would be able to live their full span of time, under as normal conditions, for them, as possible. Also, sick animals, wherever possible, would be treated, while those that could not be would be euthanized, or otherwise humanly killed, on their home ground, not taken to an abattoir.

I am also a believer in "you are what you eat." I know it would be next to impossible to prove, scientifically, that a mental state of animals, kept their entire life in cages or crowded indoor conditions, could be transferred to the people who eat them. At the same time, while a lot of negative social influences affect the populations, more specifically in the U.S., where more and more people are being mentally oppressed, if not crushed by them, part of the cause there is likely their food, as so much of it comes from the "mass production agribusinesses," which is a part of the reason so many people there feel trapped, or caged, just like the animals who are the source of their food. This simply will be unacceptable in the future.

GREENS AGAINST DEHUMANIZATION

Perhaps you have heard of Luddites, the textile workers in the early 19th century England, who used to destroy equipment in the "satanic mills," as they used to call mechanized spinning and weaving mills. They rebelled this way, because these factories took away their qualified, well-paying jobs as crofters, and turned them into mere appendages of fast, noisy machines, that, in turn, dehumanized them. And back then, some 200 years ago, people had more sense about the transformation their daily lives were undergoing than today, when mechanical, routine jobs, defined as dehumanizing, became the 'norm'.

While this trend started in the 19th century Britain, it really took off with the American style mass production lines, in which the former work of qualified tradesmen was subdivided into tasks that could have been repeatedly performed by anyone. But as the companies grew and merged, even the white-collar jobs, like bookkeeping, when carried out on mass scale, and reduced to its specific aspects, were becoming a form of drudgery. And from what I can gather, so can be the work of a run-of-the-mill computer programmer, which likely is the reason why about half of those projects fail, according to the reports, or why even Microsoft programs are such a mess they have to be continually updated, as do Norton's protection programs.

Then there is the very presence of the countless electronic gadgets, from cell phones and tablets, to computers and TVs, mainly their effect on human mind. To be more specific, their negative effect on memories, imagination and thinking capacity, on reconstituting our minds on a noticeably lower level, especially in the regions that are really important to us as human beings, namely the ability to use words to express and define what is on our minds, the extent of our general knowledge, or the ability to do basic arithmetic in our heads.

Even before the above ideas, concerning mainly computers and cell phones, were summed up by Nicholas Carr in his book *The Shallows*, people started noticing, years earlier, the negative influence of TV on student's ability for abstract thinking or, in the opposite case, how the absence of TV had improved the students' language skills.

Furthermore, just living in one of the contemporary mega cities, and/or working for one of the mega-corporations, is in itself dehumanizing, or even studying at one of the huge campuses, crawling with thousands of students, most of whom should not even be there, lacking the relevant mental tools. The main reason why such places are dehumanizing is simple: Any person there is but a number, once outside of their 'tribe'. The same lot, of course, befalls the customers of such mega-corporations, which includes the governments, as they all hide behind a thick wall of computers, voicemails and call centers.

Question is, what to do about the situation? Protests alone, even massive ones, will not help, as we can see from such diverse places as the U.S. and Russia, because the powers-that-be recognize the people participating in these represent only a small minority of the population. And the better off the country is, even in relative terms, such as Canada, the less inclined the population is to protest. Even in the most extreme situations, as in Venezuela, where the desperate minority has been protesting for weeks, non-stop, the government would rather gun down the protesters than to agree to their demands to step down, and allow a truly free election.

In this situation we need to go for our model into the past. An old Irish myth of "The Salmon Leap," which enabled the hero to reach the otherwise inaccessible Glass Castle, provides the first hint, as we all know it refers to going against the stream, be it the stream of water, history or times. The second hint is provided by the odd Medieval scholar, whose free mind brought him into a conflict zone with the society. Depending on their ability to handle the situation, or its absence, they either succeeded in their individualization process (not to be confused with the American 'individualism,' aka selfishness), or they became alienated from their original ideas and goals, as well as from the society they lived in, which is a form of dehumanization as well.

The Glass Castle, in our case, is the future, as the qualities of both makes them shimmer in the distance, and both are so translucent that we cannot clearly see their outline, or whether they really are there. The second example deals with the theme of ignoring the preoccupations of the time, while following one's own course, set by one's own mind and moral principles.

And here we are arriving at our home-ground. This provides a lot more opportunities for people with related goals and principles, simply because there are more people alive today and we have better communication tools. The problem is finding a common base, genuinely relevant to the future, if not to the present. The only way to do that is to conjure up the most believable concept of a human future, based not upon one of the current economically and politically correct models of it, but on the objective reality.

In summing up the climatic factors we know, thanks to the Scientific American, that by April 2017 there were 410 ppm of carbon dioxide alone in the atmosphere, but with the other GHGs this amounted to 478 ppm of carbon dioxide equivalent. Yet, years ago, when this was noticeably lower, Dr. Wigley, of the University of East Anglia, stated the global temperature would go up by 8°C to 9°C, even if no carbon dioxide was added, or self-inflicted destruction.

Since such an option, i.e. total self-destruction, is hardly worth considering, much less writing about, I will now attempt to make the future less transparent, to firm up our steps towards it.

In spite the aforementioned depletion of metals, etc., it will not be an anti-technological dystopia. In fact, the ancients, who likely knew more about human future then we pretend to, called the coming age the Age of Saturn, a god intimately associated with agriculture, and drawing on their experience, the people of the preceding era used to associate it with the life in a Medieval village. Also, the arrival of this age was expected since millennia ago, and was celebrated, in

December, from Persia, to Rome, to the Maya domain, under the name of Saturnalia. It was a time of gift giving, feasting and more importantly, of role changing, between the servants or slaves, and their masters, expected to take place for real with the arrival of the Age of Saturn.

But a village life, from any time period, obviously leaves a lot to be desired for, especially for brainier people, as most will be. Furthermore, from the very beginning of our historical era, that is from circa 10,000 years ago, till the Roman times, people preferred to live in urban settings. The village life, as we know it from the last 3,000 years of European history, was merely a survival mode, imposed by very unsettled circumstances.

In the future we have in mind here, all people will live in an urban setting, although about 90 percent of them will need to live in small towns, of circa 3,000 inhabitants, but featuring all the amenities of a small city. The reasons for that will be many, but all of them will fall under the heading: Ecological.

To start with, the bulk of the population will have to be absolutely self-reliant in food, renewable resources, energy and water, and to produce a certain surplus. Transportation will be somewhat limited, due to the shortage of all non-renewable resources and fuel, namely bio-diesel. And, without a doubt, people will want to, and need to, live close to nature.

While it is impossible for us to imagine the mode of thinking and behaviour of people with 25 percent more brains and 50 percent more neural connections would exhibit, we need to imagine they would be improved 'models' of the best of us, in their attitude towards each other and the planet. In the public life, this would have to translate into getting rid of the power principle in all its forms, starting with the political parties, unions, professional, religious and other such organizations, while ensuring people are not only qualified to be elected, but to vote as well, that they understand the complex issues mankind is bound to face in the future. Then, those elected locally would elect, from among themselves, representatives to the next level, etc., etc., for one, ten year period, and anyone of them could be recalled at any time.

The role of the Central, or Continental Government, would be threefold: Issue a set of simple, straightforward laws and regulations concerning the rights and duties of all people, as well as those intended to control environmental and climate related conditions in each community, and thus globally, and of the quality and cost of products and services. Yet, while the government would be small, its inspectors would be ensuring compliance with its laws and regulations. Eventually, the system would be working as flawlessly as a healthy body.

The Central Government would also be responsible for procurement of metals. At first, these would come from structures and machinery in abandoned cities, from useless ships, cars and railways, commercial jets, tanks, old telephone cables, pipelines, etc. In the meantime though, efficient technology, not relying on propulsion thrust, would have to be invented to carry out space mining, and to detect and destroy large space debris, because the astronomers tell us that, within a few millennia, our solar system will leave the "space bubble" it entered some three million years ago, just as we started to evolve, to re-enter the "real continuum," full of the large space debris. This, without our presence and protection, would pummel Earth life to death.

In the meantime, most of Earth's surface, not covered by glaciers, will be aforested, as the ground in such areas is circa 5°C cooler than in the exposed ones, and it will be looked after by Ecological Corps to provide a good home for all the animals living there, as well as to prevent forest fires, or to put these out, and thus to maintain the ice age conditions. Yet, there is also a chance the space defence will not be able to deflect or completely destroy some of the largest asteroids, and their fragments will impact the planet. If so, then hopefully outside of the several rather limited zones inhabited by people or, if not, such would be pre-empted and rebuilt.

The last, but crucially important detail of the future life, will be the awareness of the presence of the Cosmic Being. While there will be no Churches, as it says even in the Bible, either as structures or as organizations, (re: the elimination of all potential power based organizations), most people will likely be able to sense this Entity, so ever-present in everything, which, by then, will include the human mind. And it will be through this Entity, as Nostradamus and the Maya told us, we will be able to directly experience, or perceive, the micro world, including the viruses, and to influence them, but also the macro world, such as the dangerous space debris, as well as communicate with animals and human beings on distant planets, which will enable the Earthlings to see their world through their eyes. Yet, while this may, for now, sound like a fantasy, it used to be often a passing reality for our ancestors, and is destined to be our permanent reality, making us, finally, fully human.

DESIRABLE ACTION

Until the 19th century public politics were dominated by the monarchies and the Church, in most of the Western world, with their rule taken over by political parties, preceded in this by the U.S., which officially never had its own monarchy. While on the European continent most of the parties had a left leaning bent, or were outright socialist, as in Germany, in the Anglo-American world they were essentially always split between the conservative and the more or less progressive, (i.e. Liberal or Labour or Democratic), wings of their rather limited political spectrum, especially so, again, in the U.S. In turn this polarized vision helps to maintain the old "divide and rule" mode of governing, in which the interest of the monied class always prevailed. And in the U.S. it means especially the few people invested in the military-industrial complex, against whose influence warned, in vain, President Eisenhower in his farewell speech. Now, moving into the present, we can see the dubious results of the decades of this "divide and rule" policies, as the American and the British heads of state are floundering in shallow waters, albeit for somewhat different reasons, while many of their constituents crave a past that never really was.

In Britain, the ill-educated older generations miss the former "glory and power" of the Empire they never profited from, which is why 51 percent of them voted for Brexit. The problem is, by now the country has to import all the coal and metals, along with half of its food, while most of its key industries, generating most of its income, are foreign owned, and while the competence of its politicians, namely their foresight, seems to be either rapidly diminishing, or it may have remained the same, except the circumstances got rather too complex for them.

In the U.S. the situation is a lot worse, as the Republicans, after years and years of obstructionism, by manipulating the electoral districts and the voters, now control not only the Senate, but by more manipulation and lies managed to score victory in the last presidential election, with almost 3 million votes less than the Democratic candidate, thanks to the "dark money," which cannot be traced. The estimates for the cost of this election range from $10 to $15 billion, of which the Democrats spent only around $3 billion. The presidential campaign alone cost was $2.15 billion of which on Clinton was spent $1.2 billion and on Trump $600 million. Yet the media, owned by the same monied group of people are raising a smokescreen now, attempting to blame the Russians for manipulating the election with their $100,000. But, thanks to the Cambridge Analytica affair, it became all too evident it was Trump's own organization that manipulated up to 50 million voters. And now, every time this fake President promises to "Make America Great Again," by which most of the gullible ignoramuses who voted for him likely mean the 10 to 15 years following World War II, if anything in particular, he thinks of arming America beyond any reasonable need, or of selling arms abroad, while cutting taxes for the ultra-rich. However, as far as the real qualification of this man for the job are, the whole world is gasping at his endless blunders and lies.

Yet, this election also clearly exposes the existential flaws, or rather deep cracks, in the house of cards the Americans call 'democracy', ridiculed since 19th century by such observers as Alexis de Tocqueville and Charles Dickens, of whom the former also foresaw some of the consequences. The major ones started to emerge during the 1930's, with the availability of radio, which became an excellent tool for propaganda, with the purpose of furthering the interests of the monied class, by brainwashing the ignorant population, as their education rests in the hands of equally ignorant people running the school boards. After all, in the words of well-known PR man Edward Barneys who, as Sigmund Freud's nephew, knew something about human psyche and hypnosis, "Propaganda in an invisible government." He also changed the expression "propaganda" into "public relations," or PR. And, of course, the brainwashing became so much easier with the post-war advent of television, as in "a picture is worth a thousand words."

Also, the more ignorant the population, the more effective the propaganda becomes and, sadly, it could not find a more fertile ground then in the culturally and educationally barren America, where 20 percent of the population knows nothing even about the recent origin of their country, and a lot more still are ignorant about the rest of the world, including their neighbour, Canada, and some 6 percent are totally illiterate. It was thanks to this glaring ignorance, lies, deceptions and false promises that Donald Trump, himself a prime example of a total ignorance, was elected president, even if merely a symbol of the era and the system, a catalyst for future events. After all, he too, just like Roosevelt, has to be seen as one of the aforementioned mythological Greek "heroes," guiding history in the intended direction, as in the years to come, after a massive socio-economic crash and the subsequent conflict, associated with the asteroid impact, Americans will have to reassess their system of values, because until now, the present system only staggered from one global foul-up and embarrassment to another. The reason, again, is 'simple': Unable to grasp a sense of themselves, their 'leadership' is unable to understand any nation on Earth, while constantly projecting their 'values' into every country they deal with, misconstruing their reality and end up tying themselves up in knots of incomprehension, or miscomprehension, upon which they then act.

But as the planet keeps warming up, which affects the male mind more negatively than the female one, we can see a general decline in the leadership in so many countries around the world, as more and more 'leaders' either feel no urgency or responsibility to act in the best interest of their respective countries and people, or they act in a pretty simplistic, opportunistic, even willful and crude fashion. But that too also suggests, where applicable, the current form of democracy had run its course. But then democracy, in principle, was never compatible with hierarchically structured capitalism.

With all the above in mind, we now should finally turn our attention to the current green politics, or what there is of it. This, in Canada, consists mainly of echoing the IPCC platform or promoting the economic expansion. Certainly nothing original, nothing that could help save the world.

The best, because it is the saddest example of such 'thinking', is the recently published book, *The Climate Crisis and What We Can Do*, co-written by the well-known environmentalist David Suzuki and Ian Hanington. The highlights of their suggestions included all the do-gooder tips, like investing in renewable energy, use of electric cars, more solar panels, insulation, bicycling, and eating less, especially of meat, and buying less "stuff."

But we have discussed, in fair details, such spurious arguments, including their refutation by George Manbiot, in the chapter The State of our Planet. I am merely returning to the theme of fake hope, so oddly resembling Trump's promises, because these too keep coming back, often authored by recognizable 'experts', who obviously just read each other's books. The Green Party then follows the voices of such Sirens. And we know from the Greek myths what happened to those lured by them. Their ships crashed on the rocks, which is where we are headed.

To avoid such an unpleasant surprise, the Green Party has to plug its ears to this popular song, inspired by business interests, by turning independently to the facts, by going back to its original radical source. This source was Edward Goldsmith, co-founder of The Ecologist, in 1969, before the emergence of the Green Party. As a critic of the "reductionist and mechanistic paradigm of science" he opposed Neo-Darwinism, and influenced by mathematical theories and the holism of early academic ecologists, he wrote *The Way: An Ecological World View*, published in 1972, and co-wrote, still earlier, *A Blueprint for Survival*, addressing the evident signs of the societies' breakdown and "the irreversible disruption of the life-support systems of this planet," which became a blueprint in the formation of the early Green parties.

While his books were selling very well, their ideas were too much of a political hot potato, and the British Green Party disassociated itself from these, to be more mainstream, which is likely the reason why they are now down to one seat in the

Parliament. On the other hand, the German Greens, who incorporated within their party all kinds of related radical groups, along with their ideas, now have 10 percent of the seats in Bundestag, and even more in local parliaments, especially in the western part of the country.

The German Greens were founded on the four corner principles of ecology, social justice, grassroots democracy and nonviolence, achieving definable successes with these, while the No.1 item on the policy list of the Canadian Green Party is the nebulous Green Economy. It states, on the very second line: "Central to our policy is understanding that there is no conflict between environment and economy." This 'miscomprehension' of facts, for populist expediency, needs no comment.

There are, of course, cultural differences between the Green parties, that designate them a "light green," or green wash, such as the British and Canadian parties, via the middle, the German Greens, to the outright militant ones, such as the Deep Green Resistance or Earth First.

Unfortunately, each one of them, for their special reasons, misses the point, either by becoming a part of the system, that they then hope to gradually transform from within, for which there is no time, or in their frustration, brought about by acceptance of the current scientific dogma, they advocate equally useless, yet polluting violence, such as blowing up of pipelines, refineries, etc.

For this and other reasons, I am merely advocating that all the Green parties should transform themselves into a radical, but nonviolent Deeper Greens, as the violence is bound to come anyhow, triggered by the asteroid impact, and/or the collapse of the system. The Deeper Greens would be also motivated by four principles, albeit of a different order, applicable to the present, but more so to the future, and include the following highlights: Climate change, (re)humanization, simplification, Cosmic Being.

1. Climate change: For the present, we need to accept the inevitability of it, with the important qualifications: this climate change will save mankind and civilization, and by

delivering a new ice age will also improve our mental state. But by accepting this premise we need to start preparing for it, in order to be able to sustain and organize, at least the participating members, for a minimum of the first two critical years after the impact, by providing the basic necessities of life, as well as security.

For the future, it will mean organizing the creation of the self-reliable communities and launching a global aforestation program, designed to maintain a stable ice age climate in perpetuity.

2. (Re)humanization: Presently, the best that can be done would be to bring to people's attention at least the realization of the extent to which most of them were dehumanized by brainwashing, made worse by skewered education, along with the electronic toys, and/or inhumane treatment, plain fear of degrading existence, not to speak of the mad scramble to fill the existential void by money and "things," of being but cut off from nature, it's calming, humanizing effect. After all, for eons of our evolution, we were part of nature and need it like the air itself.

In the not so distant future, this process will start unobtrusively, by education focused on the sources of genuine human values: literature with deeper meaning, imaginative poetry, art with layers of symbols and meanings, music with melody and rhythm, history, languages, basic philosophical concepts, along with confirmed (and revised) ideas about evolution and science in general. Almost daily contact with nature and animals, along with a heap of people every child/student will know, should complete the process, culminating eventually in reflection, contemplation and discussions.

3. Simplification: A lack of foresight by the federal government led to the haphazard creation of provinces and states, and to the burgeoning bureaucracy, now quickly becoming unaffordable. After all, no country, that is not made up of former kingdoms and their separate identities, like Germany or United Kingdom, needs to be federated, wasting money on governments for 1 million people or less, not to

speak of all the boards of education, regional healthcare administrations, etc., with all the bureaucrats getting paid circa 30 percent more than their counterparts in private corporations. In other words, a simplified form of direct governance is required, along with a simplified legal system, both designed from scratch. Yet, while such issues should be raised, as a matter of principle, there in fact is no time to rectify these problems at this stage. A part of this simplification should also be our food, that has to be simple, pure and unprocessed, not loaded with preservatives, pesticide, fertilizer and antibiotics, in maximally reduced packaging, and the public should be reminded of the government's tardiness in dealing with this. Even nationalizing the health care system would simplify it, and make it more affordable.

4. Cosmic Being: At the present there already exists something called "eco-spirituality," that uncannily sounds like a reincarnation of "new-ageism," and it claims that it is a religious obligation for people to be stewards of nature, which many deem sacred, based essentially on their feelings. Unfortunately, the lot of them seem tools for mental manipulation and forming a personal power base. But as far as I know, none of these groups are talking about the Cosmic Being. As we also know from ancient sources, including the Bible, this Being does not require of us any special reverence, although it always demanded that we protect all the life on this planet, which included, above all, the existence of extensive forests. This is a roundabout argument for the future civilization, unquestionably dedicated to a lifestyle of total ecology, whose every aspect will acknowledge, and be based on, the recognition of the ever-present Cosmic Being.

To get to that stage though will require a lot more work than gearing up for the election every four years. In fact, it would require of the re-cast Green Party to give up on the next election, as it is likely to be the last one anyhow, to become an activist organization, dedicated to preserving civilization, along with the lives of its members, and wherever possible, of animals and seed stock.

This, to start with, would require a massive, door-to-door membership drive, using the Deeper Green Manifesto as a recruitment tool, but running it first as an ad in local newspapers. Instead of voluntary contributions, active members would be required to donate one percent of their annual income, for the almost explicit use of local organizations. The accumulated money would then be used to open up small "front shops," serving as a bookshop/coffee bar, office and recruitment center.

With enough members it would be possible to set up a wholesale company and "emergency stores" in strategic locations, where members could (pre)buy, at a deep discount, and public at a regular cost, all the essentials required for the coming critical period, from suitable clothing and footwear, to sleeping bags and pads, tents, to tools, medical kits, and durable food. Furthermore, caches of such food, medical supplies and tools should also be deposited in safe locations, for the exclusive use of active members.

Most importantly, whoever reads this needs to grasp the fact that the time left to achieve all of this is very short, most likely only one or two years, because anytime later would be too late not only for the endangered species, but for the entire planet, and all the life it harbours. For even if some advanced life forms were to survive the sudden switch to the Jurassic type climate, civilization and its knowledge would not. Yet, without it, as the solar system will leave the "local bubble," within a few thousand years, the remaining life forms here would be snuffed out by the constant impacts of sizeable asteroids and meteors.

And yes, while I am certain the Cosmic Being knows how that will be prevented, through what chain of events, that I know nothing about, which is why I wrote this slight book. Now it is up to you, the reader, to do your part, with all the dedication and energy you can muster. To help you along, perhaps you should repeat to yourself the two well-known lines from Desiderata, written about 100 years ago: "And whether or not it is clear to you, no doubt the universe is unfolding as it should."

GREEN AND RED

Since ancient times, these were the colours of life, of chlorophyll and blood. Even millennia ago, the huge wooden columns at the temple and library of Artemis, in Ephesus, were painted in green and red.

This goddess, if you still remember, while known as the huntress, albeit mainly of people, was primarily a protectress of the forest, and of those who lived in it, be they animals or humans, of which the latter were members of the so-called Bear Cult, who planted all the ancient forests, and who did much of the actual hunting of the people who kept trying to destroy them.

The reason for that might seem very strange today to those who grew accustomed to the notion that nature is here to serve us, which, while very 'modern', has its roots in the Bible. Yet, the Bear Cult members knew a thing or two, we, as a civilization, have long forgotten: 1. Extensive forests are a key component of the Earth hydraulic cycle, control its temperature and balance the gases in the atmosphere. 2. Where they grow, the ground is circa 5°C cooler than where it is exposed. 3. They were also aware that if man, the top predator, grows too numerous, and thus threatens the balance of nature, nature in turn, embodied in Artemis, will come to hunt him. And this is evident not only in the oldest Greek versions of the myth about Artemis, in the Egyptian, Mayan, Celtic, and Inuit sources, but in the ecological record of climatic swings as well.

While it is not easy to date the origin of this myth, the goddess name can help us to pinpoint it, as all ancient proto-European names were composite names with a meaning. In her case the name Ar-tem-is means "to fit together the cut ice." Such an event took place twice, within the preceding millennia: After the initial heat spikes of circa 7,200 and 4,350 years ago, the asteroids cooled down the planet some 5,200 and 4,000 years ago. In either case, both the warming, starvation and floods that ruined civilizations, as well as the subsequent cooling and regrowth of the glaciers in the polar regions, have to be seen as a punishing act by this goddess, for the destruction of her forests. But most likely her name refers to the major cooling of 10,200 years ago, as her Bear Cult was probably relaunched at that time. And I say relaunched, because the presence of this 'Cult' was alternatively dated to 100,000, as well as 200,000 years ago.

And in case you have not figured it out yet, this chapter is about her coming back with a vengeance, to punish people for destroying so much of her forests. In fact Nostradamus prophecies, while not making any direct connection between such, tells us that all the old world people, who have practically eradicated forests in their domiciles, starting with the Arabs, Greeks, Italians, Spanish and English, will bear the full brunt of this revenge.

Since the forests are being critically marginalized all over the world, either by eradication or fires, the planet will be given just a foretaste of the warming that would follow, before the foretold asteroid will impact, to deliver a full-blown ice age, which will indeed "fit back together" all the glacier ice that became absent, or was "cut apart," since the end of the last Ice Age.

Furthermore, because of the current scientific dogma, we are delusional not only about our evolution, but since these topics are related, about the climate as well. Thus, just because our particular bunch of civilizations has evolved during an interglacial, most of the geniuses think this is an ideal climate for human beings – which it is not, as only the odd scientist, including James Lovelock, seems to know. It is in fact the ice ages that represent the optimum conditions for all life. They provide healthier environment, as all kinds of nasties, starting with microbes and viruses, like it really warm. But ice age climates are also good for the brains, as these, aided by O_{18}, more of which is available then, grow noticeably larger in humans, and (some) animals, as was also recently realized, without anyone connecting the dots, preferring the dogma to facts.

But where the irrational compliance with the ignorant dogma would soon terminate our civilization, and us along with it, the asteroid option, after a series of major upheavals, both natural and man-made, will deliver us to the completion of our evolution.

Such a process, needless to say, cannot take the form of a miracle, but will need to be delivered by human beings, exercising their free will, one way or the other, on both sides of the critical divide, culminating in the confrontation between those whose greed and stupidity have been ruining the planet for millennia, and those siding with life, whose main goal will be to ensure their adversaries never, ever, get such a chance again, in the ages to come.

Hopefully, if you consider yourself "Green," you will be there to oppose the resurgence of the life's nemesis, but to be fully effective in this confrontation, you will need to be prepared for it. This means mainly one thing: getting organized now, as, to repeat it, there is just one or two years left before events start unfolding as foretold.

In order to get to that future, you are to know what you would be fighting for; namely a society completely dedicated to an ecological lifestyle and protection of life, as can be deduced from what is known about the real evolution of our species, and the ecological hints in the Bible.

In many respects, this too will be a "red" future, but unlike any of those from the recent past, that called themselves socialist or communist. Nevertheless, due to the circumstances people will be living a communal life and, as we will see, while all the land and all its resources will belong, in the abstract sense, to the Cosmic Being, but in practical terms to the people who will live there. They will also co-own all the major industrial facilities and credit unions.

Detouring a bit, I have to point out that communal life, even if of a rather different kind, was practiced by entire civilizations in the past. Namely by the ancient Sumerians and Egyptians, and more recently the Incas. Concerning the red flag, it was also flown by the 15th Century Bohemian Hussites, who also practiced a communal life. It too, no doubt, represented blood, of which they had spilled quite a lot, but also the blood of Christ, his spirit, or wine, meant to be drunk during the confirmation from a golden chalice, a sign of the promised Golden Age, represented in the centre of the flag. Yet, the ordinary people were denied the spirit, back then consumed only by the priests. The Hussites also formed a true egalitarian society, calling each other brother or sister, not comrade.

The society I am trying to introduce here will not be exactly egalitarian, but an organic one, whose need to practice adherence to the policy of steady state population and economy will go hand-in-hand with wage categories and price control. This, in itself, is a sound ecological approach, as in nature weather and nutrients represent a form of such control, as specific conditions can deliver only specific amounts of food. The other consideration is holistic, in viewing the body of the society as a collection of organs, tissues and bones, represented by specifically qualified groups of individuals. And no complex society can survive, much less prosper, without all of its components working in harmonious order. If needed be, the income distribution can be guided by the level of oxygen intake, going to the specific parts of a human body, representing here the society.

In this society, again, for ecological reasons, about 90 percent of the population will need to live in towns of circa 3,000 people, with amenities and lifestyle of a small city, self-reliant in food, renewable resources and energy. The reasons will include the fact that large cities dehumanize, and their sheer size only complicates everybody's daily life there, and cuts them off from nature. Just as importantly, in the future the current forms of transportation and energy sources simply will not be there.

Each of these towns will occupy, at least to simplify my calculations, an area of 7 x 7 kilometers, or 49 km², of which one square kilometre would be allocated to the compact town and the surrounding parkland, about 8 km² to fields, orchards and some pasture, and 40 km² to an open forest, home to deer, hare, pheasants, and the odd fox, as well as provide additional pasture for the local cows and sheep.

The buildings in each town will be at most three storey, with no elevators, to save electricity. They will be, with a few exceptions, all half-timbered, constructed out of local materials, surrounded by greenery and topped by greenhouses. The central, tree-lined square will feature mainly public style buildings, some of which will be of a soft stone, such as the local live theater/music hall, library/art gallery, which likely would also house a small multiplex cinema. Other buildings there would include a school with a gym and a swimming pool, available to the public, a general office building and a hotel. The rest of the buildings facing the square would feature restaurants, cafés, relevant stores, and craftsman or tradesmen shops on their ground floors. More eating places would be situated in residential areas, and all people would eat there at a very nominal cost.

In spite of their Medieval appearance, inside these buildings the apartments would be as modern as any today, and likely more spacious. For example, a typical family apartment for four people, (re: steady state population), would consist of a large living room, four bedrooms, (as we all need our private headspace), and 2 1/2 bath, but no kitchen, in any of them, as the steel that would go into making all the appliances, sinks and pots, would be a strategic material, in critically short supply by then. This also will be the reason for so many restaurants, that in turn will provided the needed jobs. The dearth of metals would necessitate that even the central heating elements be made out of ceramic, plastic, or a tempered glass, as well as all the bathtubs, faucets, etc.

The days of private televisions, not to speak of other electronic toys, due to their negative effects on human mind, along with the fact that all locally used electricity would have to be locally generated, would be the thing of the past. Even today's radios would be replaced by receivers that would deliver programs carried by fibre optic wires, like telephone, and could likely also serve as one, as well as a kind of audio encyclopedia, or use a very small mono-colour screen powered by a solar cell.

The 8 km² of farmland, which equals 800 hectares, or 2,000 acres, would have to be able to produce more than enough wheat and other grains, of potatoes, sugar beets, canola, hemp, hops, hay, etc., for local consumption and trade. In addition, the rooftop greenhouses will produce not only plentiful fresh vegetables year-round, but also tropical fruits, coffee, cocoa, tea and spices in season, and as relevant studies demonstrate, it would take such a population only a few days to accomplish all the tasks associated with procuring most of its food, using only manual tools, which would be the case, while only a limited number of people would need to look, year-round, after the animals on the farm and in the forest, or work in the rooftop greenhouses.

This also means that much of the regular work would have to be shared, to keep people physically occupied. This, in turn, would mean they would not need to work more than around 24 hours a week, especially in the service industries, where most people would find employment. The rest of the time they would be free to commune with nature or each other, read a book, enjoy their hobby, etc., etc. Or volunteer for a year to plant and maintain forests around the planet.

If such prospects fail to define your concept of work, your thinking is too contemporary, and you need to bring to mind the fact that, until the 19th century, when close to 90 percent of the population, in continental Europe, lived in villages, and if one was to average out their yearly workload, on a per day basis, it would come to about 2 to 3 hours, most of which were 'clocked' during the summers. And, barring critical situations, they always had enough to eat, to buy what they needed, or they made it themselves, or they bartered. The reason for that: the land was theirs, or they paid a tithe in form of their crops to the lord, and having built their own homes, these too were free of rent or mortgage.

In this scenario the situation is similar. The land will belong to the people, with no encumbrances. They will build the towns and their infrastructure themselves, using local materials, and whatever they will need in other supplies and services, such as spinning and weaving their flax and wool, they will initially pay for in food, yet eventually they will also receive their shares in the factories' cash profits. After all, every economic system is essentially artificial. Only this model would serve well at least 99 percent of the population and they would make it work, just as today the 1 percent is making their model work, for now. With the largest three or four cities, featuring populations of only 50,000 people each, this setting perhaps might seem a bit too rural, at least to some of you, and up to a point, you would be right, as until the Medieval times the future was expected to be such, as already noted.

This expectation was based upon the belief in the cycles of various durations. This ranged from the Zodiac of to 24,800 year cycle, to the 12,000 years of the Indian Mehayuga, to the (nominally) Chinese twined cycles of the flowering and fruiting of civilizations, of 3,000 years duration each, and the Phoenix cycles of cultural makeovers that, on average, take about 500 years. Furthermore, people also used to assign certain qualities to periods of uneven length, bearing the names of the old gods. The still current one, designated as the Age of Jupiter, was known for its folly and frivolity, as was the god representing it. In the present period all of these time cycles are reaching their terminal point, after which new cycles are supposed to start, by ushering in the Age of Saturn.

This, as we already discussed, will commence with a major socio-economic (and climatic) flip, but, what is more pertinent to our situation, the Age of Saturn was envisioned, during the Medieval times, as rural, or drawing livelihood and resources from the land. In this respect, mankind's future will indeed be an updated version of the past.

However, the symbology that makes up the idea of Saturn is a lot more complex, if not to say convoluted, to associate him exclusively with rural life. This single entity was a god of generation, dissolution, periodic renewal, liberation, agriculture, wealth, as well as the god of the former and the future Golden Age, which rather smacks of omnipotence. His main symbol though is this scythe, and that, in his case, has more than one meaning: harvesting the agricultural crops, as well as the human crops, with an eye on planting a future civilization, which would make him an agent of social evolution. This is further confirmed by illustrations presenting him wearing the veil of the hidden divine law. This way the scythe has to be seen mainly as an instrument of death, and would also explain why his wife's name was Lua, which translates as destruction or dissolution, and why he was also known for devouring his children.

The god of the present era, since the Roman times, is Jupiter, known for craving power and wealth, frivolously displaying both, is the 'son' of Saturn, whom he exiled, according to the geographic description of Roman authors, to North America. The asteroid impact, orchestrated, as Nostradamus tells us, by the Entity we know as the Cosmic Being, will again trigger Saturn and Lua, as it were, into their deadly activities. Yet, after the brief revolution here, Saturn will reign the world, from his North American seat, for the next 7,000 years, bringing the entire world into a permanent Golden Age – a fulfilment of the promise of Saturnalia, that used to deliver an outburst of freedom, joy, and a reversal of positions between masters and servants.

While all of this likely sounds weird, if not alien, to most readers, it still points in the same direction, as do all the other predictions, and most have originated from the same source, only got more scrambled. You just need to keep in mind that, barring the odd exception, most of us are conditioned by our culture, to one degree or another. The proof always is in the pudding, or how the future events turn out. But, over the years, I have found enough evidence, scattered here and there, to convince me of the validity of the body of these predictions, and just as importantly, they make ecological sense.

So, returning now to the future at hand, we can conclude that people will live a very satisfactory life on this planet, for millions of years, as even Egyptians used to say, lacking the concept for billions, finding ways to overcome life-threatening situations, with the help from the Omniscient, and a lot of diligence.

The first on this list of things to do will be to protect all inhabitants of this planet from annihilation, after the solar system leaves the safety of the so-called "space bubble." But by then mankind will have adequate space going technology, not only to deal with this threat, in an ongoing fashion, but also to provide sufficient supply of metals for the civilization. In addition, it might also need social structure that is able to adjust the population level, downwards, by up to 25 percent to 50 percent, within a generation or two, if faced with a critical threat to the planet, construct extensive shelters deep underground, and be ready to heal the injured planet if needed be, with the help from genetic banks. But that was also the sole reason why mankind was evolved – to be the immune system of the Earth's body of life, and to do what immune systems do for their host's body.

UNCHARTED WATERS

Everyone is familiar with the saying about the inability to see the forest for the trees. This applies to the media more than most. Smothering us daily with an avalanche of words and images describing and speculating about the current events, usually of the most violent kind, their commentators fail to notice they are portraying an ever worsening social situation, which is a lot less visible that the climatic situation. Unfortunately, hardly anyone is aware of the connection between hot weather and humans, especially the men's mental state, although the connection was known for years, and written about. For example, when the hot wind blows into France from the Sahara, or in California from the desert, erratic and violent behaviour rises and, of course, all the riots in the U.S. took place during the summers. The same applies to all the problems in Africa, India, Pakistan, etc. Furthermore, as was recently revealed, by 2100, with the atmospheric CO_2 at 800ppm, the human mental acuity would decline by 21 percent, but it also means that, averaged out, it is already down by about 5 percent.

Now, with the global temperature on the rise, not only are the summers longer and hotter, the higher global temperature is likely capable of influencing the more susceptible male minds year-round, as can be seen from the dubious actions of 'leaders' that include a number of African henchmen, but also the Presidents of the Philippines, Turkey, Venezuela, and of course the USA, as well as the balmy English politicians. And perhaps even Chancellor Merkel, who always wears pants.

Yet, while dictators are not exactly unknown in modern history, they were active mainly during the transformative decades around World War II, when the West was in social and economic crisis, thanks to the meddling of the British and American plutocrats. The situation today, upgraded into a global one, is a lot worse, mainly thanks to the American meddling.

After all, the American permanent, but ever escalating social crisis, lead directly to their substance abuse crisis, and this, in turn, to the global one. And their military/industrial complex driven foreign policy kept poking at the ant hill of foreign 'opportunities', which ultimately led to the phony war with Iraq, and this then to the formation of Al Qaeda and of the so-called Islamic State and the terror campaigns. This, in turn, also made possible the war in Syria, triggered, as noted, by the global warming, for which the money bags are to be blamed for as well.

Now, to add an injury to the insult, the "dark money" had managed to buy the American presidency for their witless puppet, at least in part thanks to Cambridge Analytica, that manipulated up to 50 million U.S. Facebook accounts to help Trump win. And he, as you might have noticed, in spite his ignorance of things military, or anything else, is always in proximity to a former general or two, which is hardly a coincidence, considering the influence of the ever-present military/industrial complex, and he is fomenting the reasons to keep increasing its income.

This complex obviously expects to make a 'killing' out of the presence of their man in the White House. But if the respective individuals were hoping for some kind of 'limited' war on the Korean Peninsula, they have likely miscalculated, for if one of the renewed military 'exercises' was to turn into a full-blown attack on North Korea, the Chinese would likely again step in. After all, the North Koreans justifiably wanted a peace treaty and a removal of thousands of American 'nukes' from South Korea, which the U.S. is unwilling to deliver on. But even if such a war did not evolve into a full-blown nuclear war, America most likely would hardly ever recover from the tremendous losses in man, equipment, and military bases, from the reparation cost it would have to pay, being the aggressor, not to speak of the almost $1.2 trillion it would have to re-pay, eventually, for the Chinese loans. But hopefully, the American generals are aware of the odds of such a full-blown conflict. This certainly would not be the cake walk the Iraq war was.

Still, the danger would continue to exist in the U.S., for as long as the current regime there will endure, which is yet another reason why the current state of affairs will be terminated in a rather near future, before the warped minds there could make a bad situation even worse, by triggering World War III, in which the losing side, that would likely be the U.S., even according to a recent Rand Corporation report, that would resort to using nuclear weapons, as they were contemplating in Vietnam. Yes, such a war would also trigger a new ice age, and directly or indirectly kill billions of people, but the world would never recover from this cataclysm. Thus, in this respect as well, the coming asteroid impact will be a saving grace, even if it is bound to make us sail into uncharted waters, which we are anyhow.

Entering such waters always meant encountering unexpected dangers and opportunities, as well as new knowledge, which then led to social changes. The future we are about to enter represents such uncharted waters, or the blank regions on the mental map of our existence.

Such a conclusion, of course, contradicts the predictive ability of the current sciences. Yet, as I demonstrated, over and over, such an ability applies only to basic chemistry and physics, certainly not to ecology and human evolution, nor to the rest of the modern sciences, and much less so to history.

That, though, does not prevent the extreme nuts among the scientists and technologists from talking about a hyper-technological future. But while talking about that, they omit explaining where all the non-renewable resources are supposed to come from, as these are expected to be nearly exhausted by around 2050. And neither they bother explaining who would pay for the hyper expensive space elevator, along with the rest of the equally expensive space going technology and mining, and we are talking about $ trillions here, with all the governments busted, as the up and coming technology would eventually put at least 75 percent to 80 percent of people permanently out of work, and the mega corporations would pay no taxes to speak of, nor would the ultra rich, who ultimately would become the sole customers for most of their own goods. And, of course, in spite of the current pretensions, they never will be rich enough fast enough, to finance such hyper expensive schemes on their own.

The future, however, always turns out differently than the mighty rulers of this world expect it will, in spite the fact it favoured so many of them for centuries, just as it did for others before, in the preceding cultures. But this time, it will be very different, as the tree of our evolution has grown awfully tall, and the rotten branch that they, along with their minions sit on, will break and fall into the abyss of time below, taking most of them along.

Those who will survive, among the scientists, will be shocked to see their 'theories' crumble, as they will be proven wrong on about everyone of them, starting with the one about the frequency of asteroid impacts, the speed of the climatic changes, of the human evolutionary transformations, and eventually about the existence of the real God, we call here the Cosmic Being, and the rediscovered ability that will enable people to communicate with this God, as well as to know if someone is lying, which would change the judicial system too.

As at least partially explained, mankind's future will be anything but futuristic, yet living there will be easy, most of the times, with very adequate creature comforts, and much more advanced in truly human terms and qualities, that we would recognize as empathy, self-discipline, all pervading sense of cooperation, the basic 'building blocks' of matter and life.

While the everyday technology will be as simple as possible, just like the social organization, in order to avoid the snowballing complexity and its consequences, there will be computers, of course, where absolutely needed, along with some fully automated production facilities; to protect people from noise and physical injuries. Eventually, and with international cooperation, space going technology will be developed, that will serve to defend the planet from the dangers it will encounter in space, as well as for space mining and transport of metals to Earth, all delivered on a non-profit basis.

However, mankind's main goal and purpose will be to maintain the optimum viability of the planet, which will include maintaining the ice age conditions, and when needed, quickly repair any damage. In this respect, our evolution will upgrade us from lowly predators within the Earth's body, to its second smartest organ. The immune system.

Getting to that stage though will definitely not be easy, nor painless. The main reason is the current size of the human population. As was known for some time, the Earth can support, indefinitely, only 1 to 1.5 billion people, and some say even less than 1 billion, not 7.5 or 9 or 10 billion. And the global population will be reduced to the required level, mainly involuntarily, over the next five decades or so. In stages, but consistently.

There are vague hints of such a drastic reductions even in the Bible, The Revelation section, and appalling details of it in Nostradamus, who also commented on his shock, concerning those. But that will be the only way to save mankind and it's civilization, to usher in the new ice age.

Yet, in North America the population will fare relatively well, as circa 1/3 of the people here can be expected to survive, boosted by millions of refugees from ravaged Europe, according to Nostradamus.

This migration wave though will be preceded by a brief civil war, according to the same source, that will turn the current socio-economic system upside down, followed, obviously, by a quick rebuilding, as only a well-functioning society will be able to absorb so many refugees. Their influx will likely also flip the racial balance in favour of the Caucasian population. Yet, even here, over the centuries and millennia, will rise a new amalgam race, albeit still predominantly with Caucasian features.

As of the 22nd century, by our accounting, the entire world should be on the mend, and one of its major holidays possibly will be a new version of the Memorial Day, but more akin to the ancient "ancestor worship," in which the population will give thanks to their ancestors for their endurance, while also commemorating their suffering, over the roughly 1.5 million year long ordeal of our evolution, in which the transition stages were more like the gladiator games. The fittest in this 'sport' had to be fit, at least up to a point, not just physically, but also mentally, and one can even say spiritually, in their cooperative attitude towards nature and each other.

In the initial stages, it would seem, the number of such people would have been rather small, and to maintain the species, those less 'fit' had to survive as well. And that, possibly, was the reason why the current population was allowed to reach such astronomic levels: to enable those deemed fit for their role to form a majority of the future population. After all, in one of his quatrains Nostradamus warns that the guardian "mastiffs" will have to remain on guard, implying that, as always, some of the undesirable 'species' will survive.

This, in turn, suggests something about the intricacy of the human mind and character. Namely that we need even the less savoury aspects of it for our survival. For example, aggressivity and a burning desire, which can be made to serve all kinds of purposes, if not properly channeled, as I imagine they will be, given enough time. And there certainly will be enough of that, as was known millennia ago, but eventually forgotten.

In either case, what is coming, is the archetypal fight between good and evil, between the forces defending the rights of all life to exist, and those who, in their limitless voracity would exterminate it, in so many ways, that do not apply only to the worst of the plutocrats, but to entire nations and races, who have been practising it for millennia. So, choose your side well, and very carefully.

AFTERWORD

Right now we are all experiencing two sets of realities. The everyday reality that comes from contacts with other people, technology, animals, or any other living thing. The other reality we perceive is conceptual, as people view the world either through the eyes of science or through the eyes of the Christian God. Curiously enough, both of these views have similarly short time horizon for human role on this planet, and both allow for its exploitation.

While this skinny book, in most respects, combines the ideas of science and God, this God, the Cosmic Being, did not create the universe and all the life on Earth, but became the universe and the life. Viewed this way, even our experiences of reality fuse into one, becoming whole, with certain modifications of current scientific concepts.

If we were to recap, briefly, the entire sequence of events, we would see this: eons ago, in the process we will never understand, the latent energy of the Infinity acquired consciousness, and over more eons knowledge, we could not grasp either, which should tell us, and the scientists, about learning how to eat a lot of humble pie. At some point this Primordial Energy, 'feeling lonely', as the myths say, decided to transform a part of Itself into the universe we know, aka the Cosmic Being, and to create life there, wherever possible. And this plan, if we can call it that, ran on time like a German train, ever since. Of course, it also ran a lot faster, as the organization of galaxies and evolution of life are concerned, if such were left to natural, or accidental forces, as astronomers know, and advanced life most likely would not happen at all, within the lifespan of the universe, as some biologist acknowledge, had it not been for the Cosmic Being.

The evolution then happened more or less the way the science tells us, with one major difference: it was guided, step-by-step, by the Cosmic Being, and it was, and is, centered on cooperation, not competition. After all, even the Cosmic Being 'cooperates' with the Premordial Energy, and while it might not seem so, even the predatory creatures, which includes the birds, in a holistic fashion also 'cooperate' with their prey in maintaining life on this planet, through a process called homeostasis.

The other major glitch is in the concept of evolution of our own species. As noted, within the last 12,000 years, we ourselves have experienced two major modifications of our craniums, and if the global warming was to intensify, we would experience at least one more regressive modification, as already predicted by scientists. Yet, people must have experienced the same roller coaster of changes in the ages past, but the anthropologists are unable or unwilling to see it, focusing only on the human remains that fit their dogma, while ignoring others. Besides, they have dealt with remains of only a tiny fraction of one percent of all the people who had ever lived on this planet, which includes just fragments of the really old ones.

Also, one cannot realistically expect any "hard evidence" of civilizations that existed hundreds of thousands of years ago, nor from the one that completely decimated the planet, just over 25,000 years ago. As it says in the Bible: "from dust to dust," even for civilizations, within several millennia, as the TV series "After Mankind" demonstrated.

And the same 'scientific' view applies to the understanding of climate, including, of course, predictability of its changes. As noted, climate is a chaotic system, not an incremental one, as the 'experts' keep implying. And this is evident whether we go back thousands or millions of years. In fact, no major change in nature took place gradually. At least not in the absolute sense. Of course, there is always a gradual buildup, but the changeover is swift and massive, as was the extinction of dinosaurs, followed, millions of years later, by equally 'sudden' emergence of a variety of mammalian species, all originating from the almost mythical shrew. Nor was the emergence of the universe gradual, but virtually instantaneous, after eons and eons of build up to the moment. The same applies to the consequences of such massive changes, as every living species has the tendency to linger. This can be demonstrated best by the evidence of pterodactyls and brontosauruses surviving into historical times. The former in native stories and petroglyphs in

North America, and the latter in an illustration from ancient Egypt and stories from equatorial Africa.

In other words, while most of the observations and reasoning conducted by scientists are correct in themselves, their conclusions are swayed by unsupportable dogma, which in turn warps our perception of reality. This warped perception of reality, in which everything is accidental, enabled the plutocrats, who fancy themselves the most fit to survive, to launch the current assault on life the planet harbours, as predicted by the Cosmic Being.

Concerning the scientific fallacy, we only need to go back to the metaphysical claim, still maintained by the body of science, insisting upon the Big Bang, which allegedly started by a spontaneous emergence of a tiny speck of energy. Then, during its miraculously instantaneous expansion, 99.9 percent of its particles and quasi anti-particles had annihilated each other, yet, those that remained formed up to 500 billion galaxies, each with circa 200 billion solar systems. All that out of an infinitesimal fraction of a tiny speck of energy, while from the still 'leftover' hydrogen the entire universe could be created ten times over. But still, scientists are taking this utter nonsense seriously, rather than considering seriously existence of the Cosmic Being, as our more advanced ancestors did, and who, talking of the same original state, offer the idea of an energy (mem)brane, being somehow activated.

And it all boils down to the fact the scientists cannot grasp the concept of the Cosmic Being, who, as a part of a Supernatural Being, or Primal Energy, and subject to natural laws, is not a magical being, like the biblical God, made so by the ignorant authors of the Bible.

So far, we have lived in an "alternative reality," for millennia, and our idiotic travails will continue, until we are ready to accept the true reality of our fate and undertake the tasks associated with it, namely taking care of all the life on this planet, which is the only way the Cosmic Being wants to be acknowledged, or 'worshipped'.

Towards that end, we all will have to become Deeper Green ecologists.

THE DEEPER GREEN MANIFESTO: CLIMATE CHANGE IS UNSTOPPABLE

- The climatologists have pretended, for decades, theirs is a predictable Neo-Darwinian science. But being chaotic by nature, it is not. Then, in 2016, the global temperature jumped, by 0.3°C, to almost 1.4°C. And that was the year after the Paris Agreement was signed, promising to prevent the global temperature from rising by no more than 1.5°C to 2°C.

- Yet, even if this Agreement was fully implemented, the atmospheric level of CO2 would reach 675 ppm by 2100, and with other GHGs 800 pm of CO2 equivalent. Without any meaningful action, which is more likely, CO2 would climb to 910 ppm, and with other GHGs to 1,100 ppm.

- Then there is the ignored impact of methane, bubbling up from the frozen clathers off Siberian coast, due to cause sudden global warming, at any time now, producing climate predicted for the end of this century, or much worse.

- Also, the Amazon forest, that absorbs some 20 percent of CO2, is bound to go up in smoke, within years, adding a lot more of it to the atmosphere.

- When we add up all the above, the very near future looks pretty bleak. Then comes the body of the American science organization, revealing that human intellectual capacity would decline by (further) 21 percent, when the atmospheric CO2 level will reach 800ppm, which in fact can happen any time now, thanks to the methane.

- The main body of climatologists, in abeyance of their dogma, also pretend the Ice Age ended gradually, but unsure whether 12,000 or 10,000 years ago, when, in fact it ended suddenly and cataclysmically, some 15,500 years ago. They also refuse to acknowledge the planet was so devastated, it took our ancestors 3,600 years to revive it, when the heat spike, that started 11,700 years ago, destroyed most of what they did. Furthermore, during its 1,500 years long period, the human cranium was reduced by 20 percent, as anthropologists started to realize, without knowing why or exactly when.

- Just as interestingly, all three major climactic swings were terminated by impacts of asteroids, up to 11 kilometers in size. While aware of them, the climatologists never place these in the proper context as that would defy the Neo-Darwinian dogma, as such a series of 'lucky incidents' clearly points to an intervention by a higher power.

- No, not the biblical Yahweh, but the Cosmic Being, recognized by quantum physicists as the quantum Entity that *became* the universe and all it contains. And this Being was able to do that, because it knew the entire future and possessed inconceivable calculating powers, when it emerged, which enabled this Entity to overcome mathematical impossibilities associated with guiding the evolution of matter and life.

- The Egyptian Hermetics, who call this Entity Atum, defined it almost the same way that the quantum physicists do. Yet, our still more remote ancestors claim they used to be able to receive communications from this Omniscient Being, until about 12,000 years ago. This told them about the fate of mankind for the next, yes, 12,00 years. At the end of this time, or about now, mankind will gamble with its existence, but will be saved from self-destruction by a yet another asteroid.

- This one will restore the planet's life supporting capacity, by reducing the human population to a sustainable level, of around one billion people, while also delivering a new ice age, as that creates the optimum conditions for all life. Furthermore, a 'new' human race will start to be born, 40 years after the impact, restoring our brain to its previous size and capacity, at which stage our 1.5 million year long evolution will be completed.

- North America, after a brief civil war, that will turn the current socio-economic system upside down, will then lead the world, along its path of total ecology, for the next 7,000 years.

BIBLIOGRAPHY OF RELEVANT TITLES

Isaak Asimov & Frederik Pohl – OUR ANGRY EARTH: As Mr. Asimov writes in the Introduction: "This book," published in 1991, "is not an opinion piece. It is a scientific survey of the situation that threatens us all."

Andrew Bacevich – THE LIMITS OF POWER: Former colonel, now a professor of history, the author provides a searing critique of the American society, its way of life.

Michael Baigent – ANCIENT TRACES: The evidence behind these many unexplained "traces" must be upsetting to the hard-core Darwinians.

Ian G. Barbour – WHEN SCIENCE MEETS RELIGION: True to its title, this book is examining the broad spectrum of connections between the divine and our world.

Mario Beauregard & Denis O'Leary – THE SPIRITUAL BRAIN: Very useful reading for those who believe our brains are not just a collection of "on and off" synapses.

Mark Booth — THE SECRET HISTORY OF THE WORLD: While the author provides a useful view of the few preceding millennia, normally ignored, the title is misleading, since he has no clue where and why all the mysteries he writes about came from.

Lester R. Brown — WORLD ON THE EDGE: Useful for its contents of the pros and cons, concerning both ecology and economy, albeit a bit academic.

Joel E. Cohen — HOW MANY PEOPLE CAN THE EARTH SUPPORT: A bit too academic and uncertain, but with useful details.

Paul Davies – THE 5th MIRACLE: The author, a quantum physicist, explains that life could not have evolved by an accident. A few years later he published a book titled GOD and the NEW PHYSICS: The statement, found in front, and at the end of the book, reads: "... science offers a surer path to God than religion." Yet, years later, such notions are still being muzzled.

Alan Dundes, ed. – THE FLOOD MYTH: The title is a mere semantics of usage, because these 'myths' describe, either symbolically, or in realistic details, actual events from mankind's past, that kept repeating itself.

Mircea Eliade – A HISTORY OF RELIGIOUS IDEAS: Perhaps the best title dealing with such topic. And closer attention will reveal that many of them are derived from climate related events.

Timothy Freke & Peter Gandy, ed. – THE HERMETICA: Read with caution, as it had passed through distorting prisms of millennia of waning knowledge. But it still contains stunning parts, such as those referring to Atum, aka the Cosmic Being of quantum physicists.

Jerry Fodor & Massimo Piatelli – WHAT DARWIN GOT WRONG: In spite of admitting not having the answer, the authors provide a devastating critique of the (ill)famous theory, all in the name of science.

John Geiger – THE THIRD MAN FACTOR: A useful look at the rare facilities of human mind in extreme situations.

Paul Gilding – THE GREAT DISRUPTION: A book with a lot of the right arguments about climate change and depletion of natural resources, but not so many right conclusions.

Edward Goldsmith – THE WAY - AN ECOLOGICAL WORLD-VIEW: This book will help you see ecology, and the world, in an entirely different, wholistic way.

Fred Guterl – THE FATE OF THE SPECIES: One of the most objective books, by an American author, on the seemingly inevitable climate change, by the executive editor of Scientific American.

Dean Hamer – THE GOD GENE: Real science, written by a geneticist.

Paul Halpern – COUNTDOWN TO APOCALYPSE: A list of many climate affecting natural disasters, including asteroid impacts and tidal waves, all relevant to our future.

Clive Hamilton – DEFIANT EARTH: The author is a professor of Public Ethics, and not all that well versed in facts. Yet, in spite of such drawback, it is still worth reading for its moral stand.

James Hansen – STORMS OF MY GRANDCHILDREN: If you think you still need more scientific arguments regarding the climate change, read this book by a courageous climatologist.

Edith Hamilton – MYTHOLOGY: Useful survey of mainly Greek myths, some of which contain hidden ecological clues.

Richard Heinberg – AFTERBURN: A more complex explanation of why our civilization is but a flash in a pan of our history, and the tasks that need to be undertaken to create a viable one.

Wence Horak – ANCIENT ECOLOGISTS: People left oral and written records about their millennia long struggle to maintain the viability of Earth, after the cataclysmic termination of the last Ice Age. – NOSTRADAMUS DECODED: The sage himself stated the shocking and awesome roller-coaster of events, described in most of the quatrains, and triggered by an asteroid impact, in fact is aimed at our historical period. – SKY GODS & ANGELS: Somewhere between 400,000 and 300,000 years ago a civilisation evolved on Earth that went to live in the six cyclopean space habitats they constructed above the planet, which process is described in fair detail in 'myths'. While the War of the Gods destroyed these structures, over 25,000 years ago, their equally cyclopean space ships, and their UFOs, are still there.

Stuart A. Kauffman – REINVENTING THE SACRED: True to the title, it challenges all accepted scientific ideas.

J.H. Kunstler – THE LONG EMERGENCY: In a somewhat longwinded way readers are explained why they will not have the future the corporate media keep on promising.

Jaron Lanier – WHO OWNS THE FUTURE?: This computer scientist and businessman, in spite of acknowledging the all but unacceptable human cost of it, still thinks computers will rule.

Konrad Lorenz – THE WANING OF HUMANENESS: Published over 30 years ago, the concerns expressed in this book became even more pronounced now, especially so in the US.

James Lovelock – THE REVENGE OF GAIA: One of the few books that provides the needed nasty facts of climatic consequences, if we continue with the "business as usual," which is what it was, since it got published in 2006. In 2009 he published THE VANISHING FACE OF GAIA, The Final Warning. Here, in addition to a wealth of pertinent data, he also tells us the climate science is running on a vapour of facts.

Lucretious – ON THE NATURE OF THE UNIVERSE: A very useful insight into the Roman mind, and the knowledge it contained, some of which is rather 'modern', as well as relevant.

Mark Lynas – THE GOD SPECIES: What we did to the planet, by exceeding all the boundaries that sustain life. Also – SIX DEGREES: In this book he imagines the effect of the gradually rising global temperature, by 1°C, on the Earth's climate and its life.

Juan Mascaro, tr. – THE UPANISHADS: This Indian classic calls the Cosmic Being "Brahma".

D.H. & D.L. Meadows – THE LIMITS OF GROWTH: Published in 1972, this book projected, quite accurately, the timelines for population growth, as well as decline of non-renewable resources and food (on the per capita basis), but no one, in the position of power, paid any heed at all.

Anthony Milne – OUR DROWNING WORLD: In spite being published in 1988, it still contains information relevant to our future.

Richard Milton – SHATTERING THE MYTH OF DARWINISM: A vast array of scientific facts, assembled here to discredit the current notions of Darwinism.

George Monbiot – HEAT: From the period when he, a journalist dedicated to climate change, and a new father, wanted to believe that global warming can be stopped. Yet, towards the end of this book he wrote: "I know ... writing, reading, debate and dissent change nothing."

Fairfield Osborn — OUR PLUNDERED PLANET: The author of this book, first published in 1948, was labeled "the prophet of doom", for predicting a milder version of what is now actually transpiring.

Fred Pearce – THE LAST GENERATION: Indispensable details about the past climate changes, you would be hard pressed to find elsewhere.

Scott Peterson – NATIVE AMERICAN PROPHECIES: Many of these are relevant for our era.

Neil Postman – TECHNOPOLY: How modern technology corrupted and undermined the very existence of the American and other societies.

Brian Stone, tr. – SIR GAWAIN AND THE GREEN KNIGHT: A collection of Celtic myths, many with an ecological message.

Lee Stroebel – THE CASE FOR A CREATOR: When you ignore the religious references, the scientific details make it worth reading.

Dennis Tedlock, tr. – POPOL VUH: Mayan sacred book that incorporates prehistoric events, as well as prophecies.

Alexis de Tocqueville – DEMOCRACY IN AMERICA: Demonstrates how the populist system caused problems from the very beginning,

Colin Tudge – THE TIME BEFORE HISTORY: Contains many appreciable details, if you view the bulk with needed caution.

Mathis Wackernagel & William Rees – OUR ECOLOGICAL FOOTPRINT: Using fairly simple tools, the authors demonstrate that all the developed countries use resources many times greater than their own.

R.F. Walworth – SUBDUE THE EARTH: Published over 40 years ago, this book poses unorthodox questions about all kinds of scientific puzzles, most of which still remain unanswered.

Frank Waters – BOOK OF THE HOPI: Their myths remember some key parts of our distant past.

Peter Wohlleben – THE HIDDEN LIFE OF TREES: A must read for all people who recognize our lives, all lives, are inseparable from the well-being of forests.

Danah Zohar – THE QUANTUM SELF: She was likely the first person to discuss, publicly, the reality of quantum events in our minds, in the world around us, way back in 1990. Read it.

And it is also highly desirable to include:
THE GREENPEACE GUIDE TO ANTI-
ENVIRONMENTAL ORGANIZATIONS